High Performance Pickleball Academy
HighPerformancePickleballAcademy.com
PickleballTrips.com

"Shoot for the moon. Even if you miss, you'll land among the stars".

- Norman Vincent Peale

Table of Contents

Introduction

By Daniel

How to read this book: This book exists for two reasons. First is to teach you the skills and strategies that have become our proven framework for the best way to play the game of pickleball. Second, we wrote this book so you will be inspired to enroll in our online training courses, or join us on one of our exotic pickleball trips around the world.

This book aims to provide deep insights that will help you improve your pickleball game. The single most incredible thing about pickleball is how easy it is to pick up while being so strategic and layered that there is always something new to improve. It may seem like the pros immediately became 5.0 players and have nothing else to learn but believe me, it was a struggle to reach the pro level. And it is a daily struggle just to stay there. Improving means winning more games, of course, but more importantly, it is the journey and satisfaction of knowing that you are improving. It's hard work, and it takes time, but we want to help you reach all of your pickleball goals, whatever they may be.

So what makes this book different? There are tons of YouTube videos and free "How To" manuals out there. Why pay good money for something like this? First, you get what you pay for. We have taken hundreds of hours to write this book and tens of thousands more on the court to think about the most relevant and strategic content we want to provide you. We will go deeper into each shot's theory, strategy, mental side, and execution than anyone else ever has. We have struggled, practiced, and thought through these concepts daily and know they will be helpful to you on your own path.

Second, participants often tell us they loved the coaching at clinics or camps, but it was like drinking through a fire hydrant. They can't possibly retain all the information and don't have time to write anything down. When teaching in person, we tell people to take home just one or two concepts from a lesson and practice them until they become part of their game. We have done our jobs if they can improve in one or two practical ways from a class or clinic.

However, the advantage of a book is the ability to return to it numerous times. Something might not stick out the first time, but it inspires you at another point down the road. Or maybe when struggling with a particular shot and nothing else seems to work, you return to the book for guidance, and something clicks. Every coach explains things differently, so it is always good to have multiple perspectives. Hopefully, something about how we describe a particular concept resonates with you.

Allow us to insert a caveat here: This book is written for everyone but explains some higher-level pickleball insights. While many concepts remain constant from beginner to elite level, other insights may contradict some beginner or intermediate level teaching. We don't want to confuse you, but as you have likely seen, the pros don't always follow the same rules that beginner-level players do. We want to break down the strategies and concepts to help you reach the highest level possible. This is definitely not an introduction to pickleball, so if you are looking for basic rules, ideas, or strategies, there are plenty of other books for that.

Of course, the problem with a book is that we cannot *show* you the concepts we explain. In our online training programs, we actually demonstrate each of the skills and strategies outlined in this book, along with some drills we use to master the techniques. If you are a visual learner, our online pickleball course is a great companion to this book. Sign up at HighPerformancePickleballAcademy. com.

For us, pickleball has been life-changing in so many ways. From the relationships made, businesses created, better fitness, and rediscovering the fun of competing and constantly improving, it has been an incredible ride that continues today. Whether your goal is having fun, losing some weight, moving up a level, playing a tournament, or becoming a professional pickleball player, go for it. We are there to cheer you on.

Chapter 1

Life Before Pickleball

By Scott

Our pickleball journey began sometime in 2012 when a good friend innocently invited me to play this crazy-sounding game called pickleball. Of course, being a racket sports junkie, I had to try it. Little did I know it would so profoundly impact the course of my life. I am sure many of you can relate. It is amazing how one moment or encounter can change your life so much, and John Foss will probably never know how thankful I am for his innocent invitation back in 2012.

I would also be remiss to exclude my parents, who contributed significantly to my journey long before I even encountered pickleball. At 6 years old, they bought me a ping-pong table for Christmas and, by extension, a lifetime of skills, friends, family, and competition. Unfortunately, all too often, those paddles were used on my backside, but it was always deserved. I have been fortunate to share many of those same lessons and moments with my own kids and even my first grandchild, Holland.

Just as impactful, my mother took me to our country club for tennis lessons around the same time. I loved it and played through my junior years, being ranked in Texas and finishing third at state my senior year after an undefeated season (until that tournament anyway). Entering the University of Texas, I tried walking onto the team, but lost a heartbreaker for the last spot that effectively ended my tennis career. I was never happy without a racket in my hand, so I picked up racketball, which later connected me to Japan. I like to think things worked out how they were supposed to. Decades later, I met the guy who knocked me out of college tennis, when he coached against my sons' high school tennis team. Andy plays pickleball now, and we have done clinics for his club in Denver. It is so interesting how things come full circle and what a small world we live in, especially in the world of pickleball.

Many people don't know about the 16 years our family spent in Japan. Inevitably they ask, "why Japan"? Honestly, I can't say for sure. It was either an answered prayer, a mistake by the Japanese government, or just perfect timing. I had visited Japan once during college and became fascinated with the culture. Until then, I believed America was superior, but my experience in Japan shattered my worldview. I learned that different doesn't mean worse, another lesson that forever impacted my life. That summer, I made lifelong friends who showed me around Tokyo while practicing their English and demonstrating a level of hospitality I had never experienced before. All I can say is those friendships and memories drew me back.

Fast forward seven years when Susan and I had graduated from the University of Texas, married, and were living in Atlanta where I worked for a commercial real estate developer. My boss suggested joining the Japan America Society, as the Japanese were buying up and financing vast amounts of commercial real estate in the late 80s. When I discovered the Japanese government offered scholarships to international students for graduate school, I decided to apply. We always wanted to live abroad for a stint and become fluent in a second language. I was miraculously selected and received an all-expense-paid scholarship, along with a generous monthly stipend to fund a couple of years of language and graduate school, an offer too good to refuse. I ended up with a master's degree in economics focused on Japanese business and became quite fluent in the process.

Initially, we only planned to live in Japan for a couple of years (in fact, that's how I convinced Susan to go in the first place), but it turned into 16 incredible years. Daniel was just 7 months old when we moved, and our 3 other kids were born in Japan - Meredith, Jonathan, and Stephen. Most of our American friends sent their kids to international schools, but one of the best decisions we ever made was sending our kids to local Japanese schools instead. When Daniel was 2 years old, we found a tiny nursery in our neighborhood and tried it out. We were shocked that Daniel was babbling away after just a couple of months. I have to admit I was jealous because while I toiled away studying for hours, Daniel spoke better Japanese from just playing all day at preschool. As a result of Daniel's positive experience, we put all of our kids through Japanese primary and elementary school. Not only did they learn the language and receive an excellent education in fundamentals such as math and science, they also gained a completely different worldview from their American peers, essentially growing up in two cultures. At school, our kids learned everything from planting and harvesting rice fields, taking care of chickens, sewing, respect for others, and of course, perfect Japanese. As a parent, the sense of personal cleanliness and responsibility was probably the most valuable lesson they learned in school. There are no janitors in Japanese schools, so the kids clean up after themselves. If you tour Japan with Pickleball Trips, one of the first things everyone notices is how clean the entire country is. To this day, we feel like Japanese school ended up being one of the best gifts we gave our kids.

The kids didn't appreciate it at the time, but they grew to value their experiences and have all benefited tremendously. Meredith landed a flight attendant job with Delta Airlines because of her Japanese, Daniel lives there and runs a tour business, and Jon and his wife Makaya taught English in Japan for a couple of years. They complained about some aspects, like having to study English daily before attending Japanese school. And because they weren't really American or Japanese, identity was a challenge in a homogenous country like Japan. But for the most part, Japanese kids treated our kids as one of their own. One of Daniel's preschool friends even tried to convince his mother that Daniel was Japanese, arguing that he must be because he spoke Japanese and acted Japanese. We quickly realized that kids don't care about nationality, color, or race. They are just kids.

After I graduated in 1991 with a Master's in Economics from Shinshu University, we moved to Tokyo, where I worked for a market entry consulting firm. It was a great experience with numerous lessons about the world of Japanese business. In 1995, I stepped down and founded an import company called Clean Systems Japan, betting the farm (even though it wasn't much at the time) on this new venture. It was a leap of faith with so many mouths to feed. Like most businesses, we struggled for the first years. Rent in Tokyo was costly, and we couldn't afford an actual office in the city. I set up a home office, but our house was so small that I could only fit a desk in the bedroom. American clients frequently called in the middle of the night because they forgot about the time change. I must have sounded sleepy when I answered the phone because most people realized their mistake and apologized profusely. My client Jim never quite grasped the concept of different time zones, though, and woke us up on numerous occasions, completely oblivious.

Though it is the center of business and industry, the main problem with Tokyo is that 30+ million other people live there. That makes it tough to buy a house, find recreational areas, or have much green space. So after living in the concrete jungle for 6 years, we stumbled across the perfect opportunity to return to Nagano Prefecture when a former classmate offered to rent us his home in a small town called Ueda. He is a big guy by Japanese standards and built his house accordingly, so much so that people thought we must have imported the materials from America. Because of the 1998 Winter Olympics in Nagano, the government had constructed a bullet train line through Ueda, and I could commute to Tokyo once a week while working from home. I was working remotely long before it became a thing. Our house was surrounded by rice paddies, apple orchards, and mountains in a beautiful rural area. The first day of school was like the circus came to town. None of the local kids had been outside Japan and most had never interacted with anyone from another country. After the initial frenzy, Japanese kids quickly got used to our kids and treated them as one of their own since they spoke Japanese so well. Not only did we adapt, we thrived in the countryside. Within a couple of months, most everyone in town knew our house, and visitors who got lost only needed to ask where the "gaijin" (gringo) family lived.

Returning to Nagano Prefecture, we had more time for sports and activities. Our boys played tennis, volleyball, and badminton, with some occasional soccer, basketball, and roller hockey thrown in for fun. Unfortunately (or fortunately), they never qualified for the sumo team. Earlier, I attempted some Japanese martial arts lessons, but decided to protect myself with a racket after getting thwacked on the head repeatedly with bamboo swords. We also discovered that Japan has incredible natural beauty despite its reputation for being crowded. We explored as much as possible by hiking, skiing, snowboarding, and visiting hot springs all around Nagano.

Rain, snow, sleet, or hail all Japanese kids walk to and from school every day. It reminded me of my mom's stories about growing up in Oklahoma walking 10 miles to school - uphill both ways, of course. Walking definitely contributes to a healthy lifestyle, though, and is one of the reasons I believe Japanese people still have the longest life expectancy in the world. We loved the idea of walking to school but received special permission to drive our kids because we needed more time to work on their English skills. Every day before school started, we would wake them up early to work on spelling, vocabulary, grammar, reading, and writing in English. Then they would go to school and do it all over again, this time in Japanese. You can imagine the daily chorus of complaints, but we persisted. As a result, the kids now appreciate the incredible value of speaking another language. And they still got to walk home from school with their friends, getting into plenty of mischief.

Speaking of mischief, one winter day, Daniel and his friend hatched a scheme to throw snowballs down from a hill at kids walking the road below. Unfortunately, he seems to have inherited remarkable aim from his mother, resulting in him hitting a girl squarely on the nose. Seeing the direct hit, Daniel and his friend took the sensible and brave option of immediately fleeing the scene. Unfortunately, as the only non-Japanese kid in the entire school, he didn't realize that you can run, but you can't hide. We were informed by the school authorities of the incident, bought a cake to express our sympathy, and apologized to the family to restore the harmony.

We were fortunate that several Japanese people became incredibly loyal friends, welcoming us wholeheartedly into their communities. Susan often talks about when I left on a business trip, and the whole family came down with a stomach bug. After hearing about it, a gaggle of Japanese women descended on our house, cooking and cleaning gear in hand. They didn't leave until the house was spotless and the fridge full. Our kids adapted so well to Japan that Susan often reminded them to speak English at home, their mother tongue. One time in preschool, when asked about his day, Stephen asked whether he should answer "in the way we talk at home, or the way we talk at school," not understanding that English and Japanese were distinct languages. To this day, Daniel sleep talks in both Japanese and English. Once on an extended family vacation to Hawaii, he nearly scared his aunt to death when she woke up to what she thought was an "Asian burglar" in the adjacent room.

As I mentioned, living in Nagano involved us in hiking, skiing/snowboarding and occasional mountain biking.

We even bought a ski lodge in the Japanese Alps, running outdoor adventure camps, international school trips, and hosting Japanese and international clients. For me, learning to snowboard entailed a couple of the most painful days of my life, mostly spent on my backside. Daniel and I learned together so he fell too, but he had the significant advantage of being 12 years old. After a dozen enjoyable years of family ski trips around Japan and Colorado, I eventually gave up snowboarding after an incredibly bitter tussle with a tree while trying to follow Stephen through deep powder. Fortunately, a new hobby lurked just around the corner... My boys still love to snowboard together and make an annual trip to Japan. Daniel even bought a 6 bedroom house close to the slopes and famous snow monkeys, where he runs an Airbnb, outdoor expeditions, and pickleball camps.

At nine or ten, Daniel got more serious about tennis. He won the Nagano prefectural tournament in junior high, earning the right to represent the prefecture at nationals. Needless to say, Daniel was the only non-Japanese player in the tournament. He managed to win a couple of rounds, and if Kei Nishikori hadn't been training in Florida, they might have played each other.

We also started playing volleyball in Japan. Jon and Stephen especially loved the team aspect of the sport, playing for club teams year-round. The Japanese work ethic extends into sports, where even elementary kids have long, grinding practices. Gyms are unheated in winter and not air-conditioned in summer, which is also part of the philosophy. It was a great experience, and they made some lifelong friends they keep in touch with to this day. In fact, a couple months after we moved to Colorado, practically their whole volleyball team, along with parents and coaches, stayed in our house for a week. It was absolute madness, but we blew their minds with all the activities - most of them had never even been outside Nagano. Susan was exhausted from cooking for 25 people, and the kids' only bathing entailed a chlorinated hot tub, but we got through it, and they had the time of their lives.

Another sport taken seriously in Japan is badminton. I must confess that before playing competitively, I thought it mainly involved backyard BBQs with a beer in one hand. I was humbled after losing to 60-year-old ladies. I got Daniel involved, of course, and we graduated to the advanced group where we would get incredible workouts. I have no doubt that in addition to tennis, badminton played a significant role in developing our quick reflexes since it is the fastest sport in the world. I could not have foreseen future pickleball careers, but badminton definitely played a role in our path to becoming pickleball national champions.

Our time in Japan also allowed us to fall in love with travel. Because other Asian countries are relatively close, we took family vacations to exotic locations all over Asia and the Pacific. After one lame Christmas in Japan, we spent the following holidays traveling instead. In 2000, we celebrated the new Millenium in New

Zealand where we bungee jumped, heli-hiked glaciers, raced luges, snorkeled, white water rafted, and jet-boated our way through the country. It's like every Kiwi is an adrenaline junkie: we fit right in. Another unforgettable experience was Indonesia, where we visited the islands of Bali and Lombok. In Lombok, we swam in a waterfall with village kids. The local kids didn't have bathing suits, so they just dropped their shorts and dove right in. Walking through their town of huts and one-room houses was a profound lesson, making us appreciate our blessings. India was another vital lesson, where we saw grinding poverty unlike anywhere else. We visited a rescue school and heard stories of kids being sold into slavery, prostitution, or manual labor and struggled to cope with our own comfortable lives. The day spent in Delhi traffic was possibly the hottest day of our lives. We crammed into an un-airconditioned rickshaw and drove around town in choking car fumes and pollution, not sure whether we would survive.

Then there was our day in Cambodian hell. We drove for 8 hours on dusty pot-holed roads, the Cambodian driver chain-smoking the entire way. It didn't help that the kids contracted food poisoning. At one point, Stephen projectile vomited over everyones' suitcases, and Daniel had debilitating diarrhea. He paid a small fee to use the "toilet," just a hole over the river with a bucket of water for toilet paper. Parts fell off the car on two separate occasions, they tried to add a cargo of live chickens, and at one point, we hit a dog, capping off the day. Needless to say, it was an unforgettable experience. Travel really is the best education, although sometimes it's more enjoyable upon reflection than while it's happening.

Eventually, we made the most challenging decisions ever and left Japan. My import and consulting businesses had reached a point where my associates could run it, and I no longer needed to remain in Japan full time. More importantly, we wanted our kids to have some time in the American education system before attending university. When we moved to Japan, we never foresaw how it would change us. We are grateful for the fantastic experiences, loyal friends, and lasting memories we made along the way.

Moving to the States, we chose Colorado partly because of its similarity to Nagano. We didn't have any geographic restrictions and wanted to live near the mountains where we vacationed. We visited Colorado Springs, and it checked all the boxes. Even so, moving back was a daunting task. Kids grow up faster in America and can get into more serious trouble. The kids' English skills were fine, but we had no interaction with American culture besides cousins, summer camp, and an occasional movie. They didn't know any slang, pop culture references, or American music. Jon especially missed his friends and struggled with his identity. Once, he even "ran away", making it as far as the next street over. Needless to say, it was a huge adjustment for us, much more challenging than moving to Japan 16 years earlier.

The tennis team ended up being an excellent avenue for our boys to adjust. Daniel started the process by trying out for the varsity team. Before tryouts, we met the coach and told him Daniel was a good player. I'm sure he took our claims with a grain of salt - after all, they had a powerhouse team, and most parents overestimate their kids' abilities. Because Daniel was such an unknown entity, he had difficulty even finding practice partners. There was even a rumor about a Japanese kid joining the team. I became his practice partner, and despite struggling to breathe at 6,000 feet, we practiced every day to prepare. Tryouts began, and he started at the bottom of the totem pole. He slowly moved up the ranks, winning every round, beating the varsity players one by one. After winning every match, Daniel had to play everyone again, just because the coach was so shocked that he kept winning. Daniel became the #1 singles player as a junior, leading them to a state title where they set the Colorado record for the most points ever scored. He received the trophy for the team at the school assembly, blowing any previous anonymity. Subsequently, both Jon and Stephen ended up playing #1 singles, leaving a legacy of numerous state championships and many incredible memories.

After graduation, Daniel accepted a scholarship to play tennis at Azusa Pacific University. His first year, he played #5 singles and was the only American on the team (if you can call him American). After two years and a semi-final appearance at the national NAIA tournament, he decided to change gears, spending a semester studying the Middle East's religion, culture, and politics in Egypt. He visited Turkey, Syria, Israel, and Jordan, entering discussions with politicians, religious leaders, students, journalists, and filmmakers. Among his favorite concepts to this day is hacky sack diplomacy (he has since converted to pickleball diplomacy) or the idea that sports can break down barriers between cultures. I learned how independent he was when I visited him for a week in Egypt, taking him out to dinner on the Nile River for his 21st birthday. While he attended classes, I visited the White Desert in the Sahara, one of the most remote places in the world. I would have been a goner if my guides had left me, or we hadn't made it through the torrential sandstorm. Returning to Cairo, I realized that we may have taught Daniel too well, as he was now thriving in a place where I could barely survive a week.

After graduating and being elected the Outstanding Senior in the International Business program, Daniel took his first job in Nairobi, Kenya. I'm guessing you see a trend by now. He worked for a company selling fuel-efficient cookstoves to rural Kenyan families, most of whom cook on environmentally destructive open fires. Again, I couldn't resist visiting. On a safari in Masai Mara National Park, I learned two African proverbs. First, after being somewhat frustrated with everything taking so long and people constantly being late, I heard an explanation about Africans' concept of time. "In America you have watches, but in Africa we have time." Sitting under the stars of the primal African Savannah, I wondered if that was indeed a better way to view our short time on earth. Second, after a horrendous night of sleep battling mosquitoes in the tent, Daniel shared another poignant proverb: "If you feel too small to make a difference, try sleeping with a mosquito." Profound, but not exactly comforting when worried about catching malaria.

Daniel decided to stay in Kenya but quit his stable job after 9 months. He didn't like the job and couldn't handle sitting in an office all day. I couldn't believe it. At 23, he had a good salary, a furnished apartment, a maid, and a driver and seemed to be living the dream. Susan, listening to our phone conversation, whispered in my ear, "look in the mirror." I should have suspected that given his upbringing and my background, perhaps Daniel was destined to be an entrepreneur. I must have ruined my other boys, too, because both Jon and Stephen have started their own businesses after brief stints working in the corporate world. Even Meredith, a flight attendant, could never survive a traditional 9-5 job. It appears I have ruined all of our kids for conventional employment.

Let's call Daniel's ventures in Africa "learning experiences" rather than financial successes. The life experiences were invaluable, however. For example, we balked and tried to dissuade him when he decided to travel overland from Kenya to South Africa across 5 countries to meet us for a family vacation. It took him 3 weeks to sightsee, volunteer, and travel *by bus* across the continent, being conned twice, sleeping who knows where, spending over 100 hours on the road, and thankfully living to write about it (danieljamesmoore.wordpress.com). He started a chili farm in Northern Kenya with a friend, among other entrepreneurial business ideas in Africa. The idea was to generate alternate sources of income for members of the Samburu Tribe while farming unproductive desert land. I liked the vision, but the sample chili powder was so hot that even a spice fanatic like myself could only handle a tiny amount at a time. We laugh about that, as I still haven't finished the sample jars he sent me years ago.

Although I am a pickleball addict, I describe myself first as a serial entrepreneur. Over the past 40 years, I have started or partnered with over 40 new enterprises. Many failed, some lasted through a season, and a couple have succeeded beyond my wildest expectations. I have lost countless nights of sleep over the failures and mistakes, but a baseball analogy helps me keep the losses in perspective. Out of around 40 attempts, I have struck out 20 times, hit a dozen singles, several doubles, and perhaps 3 home runs, maybe even one grand slam. When things get tough, I have to remind myself that hitting around .500 isn't too shabby in business or baseball. You just have to keep swinging.

Chapter 2

The Pickleball Journey

By Scott

Sometime in 2012, my date with destiny arrived. I am, of course, talking about the day I first stepped onto a pickleball court. At the time, I had no idea of the danger I faced, the years of addiction and sleepless nights haunted by silver medals. I joke of course, but pickleball has been one of the most life-changing things to come into my life recently, and now I can't imagine my life without it.

There were no dedicated courts in Colorado Springs at the time, so we taped lines and played about once a month. I was basically just playing tennis on a pickleball court at this point, whacking away at any ball that came in my direction. I probably would have continued playing this way, but fortunately my fellow players understood the game well enough to teach me the strategy and some finer points, such as the soft game. I hated hitting soft at first and had virtually no patience, but slowly learned some strategies. I had fun every time I played, but I have to admit that I still considered pickleball just a recreational activity, not a serious sport, and I never imagined it would take over my life.

That transition began in 2013 when a friend asked me to play with him at nationals. I was skeptical about the existence of such a thing as pickleball nationals but decided to go anyway. We almost forfeited our first match, getting lost en route to the tournament and not knowing what we were doing. We promptly lost the first round, trying to hit through our opponents and making dumb mistakes. Through a combination of coaching, grit, and luck, though, we actually proceeded to win the next 7 matches in a row, making it all the way back to the gold medal match. We lost soundly in the first game, so I decided to play aggressively in game 2. We were winning but started making rookie mistakes like foot faults, missing serves/returns, and serving from the wrong position. We ended up losing, but my life had already changed. I won a silver medal, but more importantly, I briefly watched the 50+ singles tournament. I had never seen singles pickleball, but immediately knew that I could win. That day I decided I would become a national champion, no matter what.

The same day, I heard from Susan that my 91-year old father-in-law suddenly passed away. As I reflected on his life, I considered how little time we really have. I decided to get serious about training and dedicate myself to this newfound goal. I needed a hobby anyway because Stephen had just left for college, making me an empty-nester with too much time on my hands. In addition, I was rediscovering the joy of competing, something I had not done seriously in 30 years. pickleball was not just the perfect sport for me, it was also the perfect timing for me to discover it. A new chapter of my life began.

Admittedly, I caught two critical breaks in 2014 that facilitated my path to becoming a national champion. First, I met a blackbelt karate instructor who designed a pickleball-specific workout program to make me faster, stronger, and less prone to injury. I never lifted a weight in my life, was stiff as a board, and had gained about a pound a year over the previous 20 years; I was an injury waiting to happen. So for 6 months, I worked harder physically than I ever have, doing a mix of weight lifting, stretching, and cardio exercises to lose weight and build muscle. After the initial soreness, I felt stronger, faster, and more flexible after each workout. I even cleaned up my diet, reducing carbs and cutting down on my main vice, sweets. As a result, I lost 20 pounds in 6 months and never looked back.

I caught my second major break when Daniel moved back from Kenya in April of that year. I shared my vision of becoming national champions and did my best to persuade him to join me. I told him, "this is your best chance to become a national champion. I have seen the competition and know that if you train, you can win. Someday it will mean a lot to you, open doors and provide opportunities you can't imagine now". He bought in, and I had a new training partner. We started training and playing several days a week. Our routine included drilling for an hour, playing skinny singles to work on doubles skills, then playing regular full court singles.

We didn't keep track, but after the first month, I think I only won one game out of a hundred - and that was the day Daniel was sick. I have to admit it was a humbling experience. Not only was I not the best player in Colorado, but I was also no longer the best player in my own family. Although I was surprised how quickly he progressed, I never expected him to let me win, as I never let my boys beat me either. They had to earn that privilege, and all of them beat me in tennis around age 15. The difference in pickleball was that it only took Daniel a few weeks. Once on the court, I knew he had what it took to be the best in the world. Beneath his relaxed demeanor, a competitive fire appears when he competes. And he had the requisite skills to back it up.

After 4 or 5 months of these beat downs, I was ready to get out of town and play somebody else. That opportunity came in September when we headed to our first big tournament, the Tournament of Champions in Ogden, Utah. It paid the most prize money of any tournament and attracted the best players in the sport. Daniel and I teamed up, not having any pressure - or experience, to speak of. Frankly, most of our doubles experience came from playing skinny singles against each other. We had no idea what to expect. We lasted a few rounds and had some initial success, but our overall takeaway was that we had to go back to the drawing board and learn to play doubles. We still felt like tennis players playing pickleball rather than actual strategic pickleball players. Reluctantly, we admitted that success in doubles was not going to come overnight. This would take time and dedication.

We did, however, have high hopes for singles since singles pickleball is similar to tennis in many ways. I reached the gold medal match in senior singles and played well against Glen Peterson. We would later compete in dozens of singles matches, play with/against each other in numerous men's doubles matches, become both TOC and national champions together and in the process, create a lasting friendship. But whether through lack of experience or practice, he got the best of me that day. Perhaps it was a good thing because it drove me to practice even harder in the subsequent months. Daniel had a decent tournament, finishing fifth. It was his first big tournament, though, and I knew he just had to play like he did against me. We returned to Colorado even more determined to make a showing at nationals, increasing the intensity and frequency of our practice sessions. TOC must have lit a fire in Daniel because no longer was I simply losing; I was having trouble winning a point. I didn't stand a chance.

We returned to nationals in November, 2014. Daniel and I played together in both age, and open events in men's doubles and again came close to beating the top teams.

We even split sets with the team that won the gold medal but couldn't cross the finish line. Experience just takes time, and although we were improving, we weren't there yet.

After playing against Daniel every day for months, it felt like my senior competitors were moving in slow motion. I finally won my first gold medal at nationals, a significant milestone for my pickleball career. Daniel had a more challenging time but prevailed to take gold in the age event. We did it. We became national champions on the same day and achieved something we never thought possible before encountering pickleball. I was happier about Daniel winning than my own gold, but it was even more remarkable to become national champions on the same day.

The Open (prize money) singles divisions remained, so we still had work to do. Sure enough, Glen was back, and I faced him in the senior men's final. This time I was fortunate enough to come out ahead. Daniel shifted gears and beat up on everyone. We left nationals with 2 gold medals each and a legitimate claim to being the best singles players in the world (Daniel didn't even have to put "senior" in front of his title). My favorite memory of the tournament was sitting courtside for Daniel and Wes's open gold medal match. Daniel beat him several times that tournament and took the first game. When they changed sides, Wes sat down next to me, asking with a big smile on his face, "what do I have to do to beat this guy"? I shrugged, flashed a smile, and responded, "just hit the line every time."

Soaring high that night, Daniel quickly brought me down to reality (leave it to your kids to keep you humble). I mentioned how happy I was about singles and we would do better together in doubles next year after we gained some experience. His response? "Dad, maybe we should play with people our own age..." I won two gold medals at nationals and got dumped by my partner in the same week. However, after some reflection, I agreed with the logic, and we decided to find other partners, focusing on learning the game of doubles. The results surprised us both.

In early 2015 I returned to the daily grind of drills and workouts. Winning nationals in singles only increased my commitment to learn doubles and win more titles. Not only was I playing better pickleball, I felt better than ever, and I wanted to continue on my journey of pickleball and fitness to see how far I could go. Doubles is such a strategic game. I felt like I could learn an infinite amount, and it was fascinating. Mark Friedenberg (AKA Yoda) had "discovered" me earlier that year in Surprise, so I took him up on his invitation to play together. We played in a few tournaments, winning a couple in the 50+ and even a 19+ tournament (our combined age was well over 100). However, a tournament in Washington we lost proved the most memorable. Inexplicably, we beat the #1 seeds, Tim Nelson and Wes Gabrielson. Watching the video now, I'm not sure how we pulled it off. They figured us out and came back to take revenge later in the tournament, but it didn't matter. Each tournament experience was a stepping stone, and with each win, I gained confidence, knowing I was getting closer. I learned to play doubles that year because of a commitment to practicing daily and advice from people like Mark. It was a long road, but I embraced the journey with its joy and pain.

Singles was another story, where I won every single (no pun intended) senior event I entered in 2015. I was having the time of my life. I definitely benefited from practicing with Daniel, my tennis background, and being in my early 50s.

Autumn of 2015 was our breakout doubles season. Until that point, Daniel and I were known as singles players with some occasional doubles success, but we had no major tournament wins. That all changed at the Tournament of Champions. I managed to win the triple crown, teaming up with Glen Peterson and Lydia Willis, whose encouragement (relentlessness) got me to play mixed doubles. I hated mixed doubles in tennis because the only strategy involved hitting it hard at the female player. However, pickleball strategy was so nuanced that I actually found playing mixed doubles enjoyable. Somehow I was able to repeat the feat and win the triple crown at nationals in 2015, becoming the undisputed best senior player in the world.

My success, however, did not compare with the joy of watching Daniel thrive. He won gold in men's doubles at the Tournament of Champions and nationals while winning gold and silver in singles. His only setback the whole year was losing a heartbreaking tiebreaker 13-15 in singles to a new guy named Marcin Rozpedski. There was no ranking system at the time, but he became the most likely candidate for best overall pickleball player in the world. Pickleball Rocks named us the Co-Players of the Year, ending a year of incredible memories and dreams coming true.

Where do you go from there? As it turns out, in completely different directions. Daniel loved pickleball but had too many other interests to pursue it single-mindedly. He returned to Japan to work in the travel industry and spread pickleball around Asia. He taught in Singapore, Taiwan, the Philippines, and Thailand and launched pickleball in Japan, China, and Kenya. He did not wholly give up competitive pickleball, though. It was just that winning national titles and staying on top did not motivate him the way it did for me. He returned most years to play the major tournaments and won medals at almost every event for several years. Instead of training and playing full time, he spends his time growing pickleball around Asia, guiding, hiking, snowboarding, hosting people from around the world at his Airbnb, and building his Active Travel Japan and Pickleball Trips businesses. He is doing what he loves and living his dream, something I cannot argue with, even though it is tempting to think about how good he could have been if he had actually exclusively dedicated himself to pickleball.

I went the opposite direction, training and playing

even more. I played senior and 19+ events, winning tournaments all over the country at both the local and national levels. In a Grand Canyon State Games final, Wes and I beat a pair whose combined ages were around 50, proving that age is not as much of a factor in pickleball as finesse and the strategic side. Our friend, "The Beard," gave me the ultimate compliment after the match when he reminded me in language I cannot repeat here that they have age groups for a reason, and I need to play with people my own ******* age. It is a classic match, and the link is below if you want to check it out. My favorite game of the year was playing with "the Beard" a couple of months later, though, where I also debuted the dancing time out.

http://www.pickleballchannel.com/Gold-Mens-Doubles-GCSG-2016

http://www.pickleballchannel.com/us-open-2016-mens-doubles-pro-bronze

It was also in 2016 when Daniel had the idea of combining his passion for travel and pickleball into a cultural pickleball tour of Japan. I thought it was a great idea, so we put together a flier promoting our first pickleball trip. Miraculously, thirteen brave souls showed up, most of whom we didn't even know. Our goal was to give people an unforgettable experience by taking them places most tourists never visit and give them some excellent pickleball instruction. We stayed at a combination of Western hotels and Japanese inns, ate primarily Japanese food, and gave them an immersive cultural experience.

We played pickleball, conducted clinics, or played with local players almost every day. Being a tour that a 26-year old professional athlete designed, though, I realized our participants needed a break, both physically and from the onslaught of everything Japanese. Toward the end of the trip, we announced that steak and hamburgers were on the dinner menu, receiving a collective sigh of relief. Hearing so much supportive feedback, we realized we had stumbled into another wonderful business opportunity for which we were uniquely positioned. Initially, we only thought of leading trips to Japan. But when an opportunity arose to take players to the Spanish Open, we realized we were thinking too small. Daniel and I have both traveled to over 60 countries. Travel is in our DNA, so taking people around the world to play and teach the sport we loved made perfect sense.

Over the years, we have collected countless stories and memories from trips worldwide. For example, in Osaka, my Japanese business client always takes our group for dinner and karaoke, dressing them up in kimonos and giving them gag gifts. One time we were walking through a train station and realized we had lost our trip participant George. It turns out we just needed to follow our noses because he could not resist the smell of McDonald's after a week of Japanese food. Another time in Mexico, we rode ATVs to a secret waterfall in the desert, blowing people's minds. There are so many more untold stories and memories. You will just have to come on a trip to experience it yourself.

2016 ended with me going 6 for 6 at Nationals, establishing a record that will never be broken now that you cannot play in that many events. Even more meaningful was winning a gold medal in our respective age singles the same day as Daniel and his grandfather. Three generations crowned national champions on the same day will also likely never happen again and I will cherish that memory forever.

I had an exciting encounter with a professional tennis player when I met Kei Nishikori in Spain after the Madrid Open in 2016. After visiting a Spanish exchange student we had hosted, we watched the Spain Open, then taught pickleball in Portugal. Nishikori had a fabulous tournament and reached the final, where he faced a decent Spanish player named Rafael Nadal. Nishikori dominated the first set and led in the second before injuring his back and losing in a tiebreaker. Waiting to check-in at the Madrid airport the following morning, I looked over to see none other than Kei Nishikori standing alone at the check-in counter. I walked over to him and talked to him in Japanese, catching him off guard. I told him that he played great and I had been cheering him on against Nadal. He was disappointed but giddy about moving into the top 10, the first time ever for a male Japanese player. We chatted for a while, and I asked him if he knew about pickleball. He did not. I told him about it and suggested that he take it up after his tennis career. When I explained that my son Daniel was one of the best players in the world and grew up in Japan, he politely agreed that he and Daniel would make a great team. I would love to see that happen someday.

In 2017, our son Jon and his wife Makaya returned to America after teaching English in Japan. Realizing the potential (and how fun it looked), Jon joined the Pickleball Trips team. We started by leading an Italy trip together. We had a blast eating and touring our way through Italy, then playing in the Bainbridge Cup, a Europe vs. North America tournament. Playing for the North American Team against players from around the world was one of the most fun pickleball experiences ever. The cheering, friendly, competitive atmosphere reminded me of a world cup soccer stadium. Jon and I even won the Italian Open men's doubles event together. It was great to see another of my sons come into his own as a pickleball player. He subsequently took over operations in Europe and most of the marketing/finances for Pickleball Trips. I still plan some North American trips and help lead trips when needed but mostly go along for the ride and watch the boys turn their passions into unforgettable trips for pickleball players.

I have to confess that although I don't play anymore, tennis is still my favorite spectator sport. So when asked to join a charity event and play pickleball with Andy Roddick, I jumped at the opportunity. When Andy arrived, we handed him a paddle and explained the rules. He spent 30 minutes warming up (learning to play) and was ready for prime time. Kyle Yates played with Andy, while I played with Amir Delic, Bosnia's former Davis

Cup captain. In-game 1, Andy stayed back, unsurprisingly trying to play tennis on a pickleball court. He hit hard and returned shots we couldn't believe, but we still beat them soundly. This displeased Andy, to say the least (I thought I was the most competitive person I knew until I met him). The exhibition was just 1 game, but when we tapped paddles, he said, "I'm not losing to you two. Let's go two out of three". Sure enough, they beat us the next game and pulled out a tight final game, winning 11-9. Needless to say, Andy and Amir were quick learners, dinking effectively and keeping balls away from Kyle and me by the third game. They ended up sticking around and playing with the crowd for at least another hour after the event, and everyone loved interacting with them.

https://www.youtube.com/watch?v=y0kqk0ozaho&t=8s

I was also inspired by my love of tennis when I foolishly challenged Simone to play the pickleball Battle of the Sexes, as we were both the undisputed champions of our respective groups. My main problem was that I didn't realize how competitive she really was. Both the doubles and singles matches were a blast. I loved the throwback stuff we got to do along with the dance that Susan and I performed. We also had some of the most intense and fun pickleball ever. If you haven't seen it, check it out below.

http://www.pickleballchannel.com/Battle-of-Sexes-2017-singles

http://www.pickleballchannel.com/Battle-of-Sexes-2017-doubles

My 2018 pickleball highlight was winning the Triple Crown in the U.S. Open, fulfilling my last primary pickleball goal of winning a triple crown at all three major tournaments. Very few players will ever win a triple crown, as it is the most formidable feat in pickleball. You can't have a bad match, the singles day is grueling, and you and your partners have to be totally in sync. It was my 6th Triple Crown, but perhaps the sweetest, as I felt I had completed the circuit. Not to mention the fact that they are getting more challenging every year.

Even that formidable goal paled in comparison to Daniel and I winning the Bend Regional tournament that August. We beat several of the top players in the game, somehow pulling out the gold with an incredibly hard-fought tiebreaker win against Wes and the Beard. It was my favorite day of pickleball ever, as Daniel and I won our first pro-level tournament together. My only complaint is that no one taped the match. At Nationals that year, Glen Peterson and I lost 15-13 in the final tiebreaker, leaving me a couple of points short of another triple crown.

In a completely different level of fulfillment, in 2019, my son Jon had a daughter, and Holland Grace Moore stole our hearts. Pickleball accomplishments are exciting, but having a granddaughter puts everything else in perspective, reminding me that pickleball is just a game. Pickleball Trips continued to add some fantastic trips worldwide like Thailand, the Netherlands, and Ireland. Stephen, my youngest son, and I even led a group of 16 to Japan, so it indeed became an entire family business.

On the court, all good things must come to an end. My streak of only having lost 1 singles match in 5 years was broken as Paul Olin aged into my group and beat me several times. The good news is that I did manage to pull off another triple crown, this time at the Chicago Open. My best win was in Vail, where Daniel and I pulled out a bronze medal in the open pro division. We beat Dekel Bar and Adam Stone 11-8 in the 3rd game to eke out a place on the medal stand.

We were all excited about the opportunities heading into 2020. Pickleball Trips had a dozen trips sold out, and Susan and I had just bought an unbelievable lot in Colorado Springs to start building on. The year started off great as we broke ground on the house, and a couple weeks later, I was traveling around the Philippines and Thailand, helping lead a pickleball trip. Little did we know it would be our last trip for a while. We started hearing about a viral outbreak in China during that trip, and a couple of months later, we were in total lockdown.

Despite the loss and hardship around the world, we were fortunate. Although pickleball trips suffered, Jon, Daniel, and I all used this time to buy or build houses while we were stuck at home. Daniel purchased a 6 bedroom place near the snow monkeys and ski resort in Nagano and fixed it into an Airbnb. He even has room to build a pickleball court in the back, which he plans to do at some point. Jon and Makaya bought her mother's house near Eugene, Oregon, and fixed it up since their 6 months of pickleball trips in Europe were canceled. I was crazy enough to think I could be the general contractor and build a dream house for Susan. Only because Covid forced me to stay home was I able to survive it and focus exclusively on completing the project. And we finished only 3 months behind schedule. I made many rookie mistakes, but I stayed sane by realizing they were all minor first-world problems. We ended up building a much better house than we would have with a builder, as we researched everything and included our own upgrades. It was a huge accomplishment and fulfilling, but one time was enough. The number of decisions was mind-boggling, and dealing with fifty or more subs was complicated, to say the least. But we got through it..

In 2020 I was fortunate to win gold with 5 different partners, 4 of whom I had never played with before. This, even though half the tournaments I was supposed to play in, were canceled. A new friend I played a tournament with, Rich Lopez, reminds me that "it's all about the relationships," and I keep returning to that lesson when I start taking pickleball too seriously.

In another of our businesses, Daniel and I also were fortunate to sell close to a thousand Pickleball Masterclass courses, our online video coaching series. Deciding to film and produce this series just before the pandemic may have been one of the best decisions we ever made. We continue to add videos and content to the masterclass, so check it out if you are interested. A huge thanks to Dustin, the mastermind behind this project.

https://www.highperformancepickleballacademy.com

In 2021, I continued to play tournaments with varying levels of success. The problem was that my competition kept getting younger. The level of pickleball at every skill level has gone up, including the pros, and it gets harder and harder to win. I entirely dedicated myself to pickleball for 2021 and 2022, wanting to enjoy the ride as long as possible. Pickleball Trips was able to run a few trips in North America, including Montana, Belize, and Mexico. Daniel is still mainly in Japan, starting some consulting work and running his Airbnb while waiting for international travel to return. We are hopeful for 2022, feeling like there is light at the end of the tunnel for the pandemic ending.

I hope you enjoyed hearing a bit of our story. As I said, pickleball changed our lives, and we know that it can change yours. Hopefully, you take some inspiration from our story and follow your goals, whatever they may be. Cheers to your success, and enjoy the rest of the book!

Chapter 3

The Serve

By Daniel

"Serve deeper!" the yips, "that's illegal!" These might be memories you associate with serving more than something like actually having a serving strategy. You might even think, "why do we need a whole chapter on the serve? Don't you just hit the ball anywhere in the court to get to the good stuff, the actual point?" There are certainly those who ascribe to this serving philosophy. If nothing else, keeping the ball in play does raise the chances of winning the point simply by not screwing things up too early. However, I prefer to think of serving as setting the stage for the entire point. What starts well tends to end well. A deep serve initiates a chain reaction of events, beginning with a short return. In turn, this allows you to take advantage of an easier third shot and then fifth shot. At the very least, hitting a deep serve makes these shots easier to execute, raising the percentage of points won.

Even if the opponents can return a deep serve effectively, they will often be pushed back, having to rush to reach the NVZ (non-volley zone) line before the next shot. They will feel pressured, rushed and unstable, helping you win more points. Contrarily, a mediocre or short serve stacks the deck against your team from the start, guaranteeing the point becomes an uphill battle. You will win some points even with a short serve, but why not increase the odds by simply hitting deeper?

Under this philosophy, even missing a couple of serves per game by intentionally aiming deeper is worth the risk. The frustration of a missed serve is undoubtedly understandable. But as long as a higher number of points are won by serving deeper than those lost from service mistakes, the odds remain in your favor, keep going for it. This does not mean one must attempt hitting an ace serve that the opponent cannot touch. Instead, simply hitting a deep serve will lead to a short return, making the third or even fifth shot easier for your team. The purpose of a deep serve is to gain an advantage in the point. The returning team begins with the edge in pickleball because they can typically reach the NV line first, but a deep serve can flip the advantage. To accomplish this, you must change your mentality and practice serving deeper. Comfort and muscle memory are essential to improving this shot and will "serve" you well. In this chapter, we break down some aspects of service strategy that will help you think about the shot in a different way, as a setup shot rather than one to simply keep in play.

Legal Serve

The USA Pickleball's definition of a legal serve states:

- The serve must be made underhand.

- Paddle contact with the ball must be below the server's waist (navel level).

- The serve is initiated with at least one foot behind the baseline; neither foot may contact the baseline or court until the ball is struck.

- The serve is made diagonally crosscourt and must land within the confines of the opposite diagonal court.

- Only one serve attempt is allowed, except in the event of a let (the ball touches the net on the serve and lands on the proper service court; let serves are replayed).

As you have likely experienced, the point of contention almost always pertains to bullet points 1 or 2. Players either serve with a cocked wrist (not underhand) or too high (not below the navel). Enforcing a legal serve only leads to frustration and contention in recreational play. I advise disregarding illegal serves in recreational play unless the offender intentionally serves illegally or gains a pronounced advantage from their illegal serve. In other words, if the server does it by accident and does not hit a particularly effective serve, why does it even matter? After a game, you could gently remind them that their service motion might be illegal, but anything else is beyond control. In tournament play, official referees will correct any blatant infraction and hopefully, what the offending player learns in tournament play carries over into their recreational game. Of course, this is not guaranteed, but you can only do so much. You can lead a horse to water, but you can't make it serve legally.

How to Hit It

There are many different service techniques and motions. Even at the elite level of pickleball, many pros utilize a slightly different service motion. Depending on what feels comfortable, your sports background before pickleball, past injuries, etc., your service motion might change or be unique to you. Therefore, saying one specific service motion is correct or preferable is almost impossible. However, there are some general guiding principles to consider when considering and practicing the service motion.

Using the Entire Body

Using the more stable large muscles of the shoulder, torso, and legs generates more power, consistency, and control than smaller muscles such as the wrist and forearm independently. This is true of any shot in pickleball but particularly true of the serve. Utilize these smaller muscles as well but only as an extension of the larger muscles. Lock these smaller muscles in, particularly the wrist, to avoid floppiness and inconsistency. Generating power from small muscles alone is a recipe for inconsistency and injury, placing undue strain on single joints and ligaments. Imagine attempting a squat standing only on one toe. Doing it once or twice is possible, albeit uncomfortable, but repeating it over and over will lead to wear and tear or injury. Instead, employing the entire body provides a relaxed, controlled, and fluid power, unlike the jerky, twitchy motion associated with smaller muscles. Picture Tiger Woods, Roger Federer, or Michael Jordan. They have a fluid, controlled power generated from their core, using their entire bodies rather than smaller muscle groups.

Often pickleball players rely excessively on their wrist when serving to gain more spin. Spin is not bad, but attempting too much leads to inaccuracy. Instead, learn to hit a simple serve deep every time before attempting spin. Use the paddle face rather than the wrist when hitting spin to achieve more spin. Again, for utmost consistency, work toward using the entire arm, starting with the shoulder rather than just a single component. Not only does this prevent injury, but it also improves accuracy, depth, and speed. In addition to the shoulders, try implementing more of the torso. Imagine golf or tennis, where the hip/torso rotation is essential for gaining power. Using the core provides more power without necessarily having to swing harder.

Weight Transfer

A similar principle to using the entire body is weight transfer. When hitting the serve in conjunction with forward weight transfer from the back foot to the front foot, bodyweight helps generate power, driving the ball deeper into the opponents' court. This means your arms and body do not have to work as hard to attain the same amount of power, thereby improving accuracy. Practice stepping forward into the court while hitting the serve or shifting from the back foot to the front foot. Whatever the case, make sure not to step back or remain with your weight on the back foot through the service motion. If you do step into the court, make sure to step back to prepare for the return of serve coming right back.

Low to High

Swinging from low to high helps in a couple of ways. First, the lower the contact point, the more likely the serve is legal. A low to high motion ensures that the contact point is below the waist and that the paddle points downward, guaranteeing a legal serve. Second, swinging from low to high means the service typically goes higher over the net. This reduces or eliminates net errors, in addition to typically placing the ball further back in the opponents' court. There is little downside to implementing a low to high service motion.

To clarify, swinging low to high does not mean implementing an exaggerated bowling or softball pitch motion. Most pros' swings resemble something between a softball pitch and a sidearm motion. But, again, every player's swing varies. In practice, figure out what works best to balance consistency and power. Your swing should allow for a consistently deep serve into the opponent's court, whatever the motion. Speaking of power, many players worry that a low to high movement eliminates the possibility of hitting hard serves. Not true. Using weight transfer and the larger muscles, generating power from an underhand service motion is attainable.

One helpful tip to ensure an upward swinging motion and more accuracy is keeping your elbow as close to the body as possible. Relax the shoulders and emulate the motion of a pendulum. Not only does this ensure a legal serve, but it also increases accuracy by decreasing the number of factors that can possibly go wrong. If your serve feels inaccurate or players often question its legality, try keeping the elbow closer to your body. Keeping it simple is a lesson I try to remember for every shot. "Perfection is achieved, not when there is nothing more to add, but when there is nothing left to take away."

Aim Higher

Like hitting from a lower contact point, consider aiming higher to improve service depth and reduce net errors. Most players aim too low, typically a foot or two over the net, meaning more net errors and the ball bouncing around the middle of the opponents' court. This makes it easy for them to hit a deep return and move forward to the NVZ line, setting off the adverse chain reaction discussed previously. Instead, to reach the NVZ line simultaneously or preferably even before the opponents hit a higher, deeper serve. Many opponents cannot return a deep serve far into your court, allowing your team to take advantage by reaching the NVZ line before the returner. As discussed previously, one way to do this is to swing from low to high. Another way is to change the paddle angle to face higher or more open at the point of contact. By changing the paddle angle slightly, you can serve deeper with better results without swinging any harder or changing the service motion. Continue adjusting the paddle angle according to the serve depth to get a feel for the perfect paddle angle for you.

Service Placement

Deep is the operative word when serving. Typically, there is an inverse relationship between the depth of the serve and the depth of the return. In other words, after hitting a deep serve, the return typically comes back short. Contrarily, a short serve is often followed by a deep return. Many players serve short because they fear the negative consequences of hitting the ball out. In reality, if you can win more points by hitting deep than you lose by hitting out, you have gained a strategic advantage, and therefore it is worth the risk. Loss aversion means it feels worse to lose a point from missing a serve than the equivalent good feeling of winning a point from a deep service. We have to overcome this human tendency to continue making ourselves hit deeper.

Attempt serving deeper and observing the depth of the resulting return. Did you win the point directly from the serve? Did you win the point as an indirect result of a deep serve on the third or fifth shot? How many times did the serve go out? Keep track of these statistics in some recreational games, and you should start to see how serving deeper results in more points won. Because there are no lines on the court where you should be aiming, count a deep serve as one where the opponent must hit the return behind their baseline. Visualize this goal when serving and aim there to increase service depth. Even if many serves go long initially, getting into the habit of hitting deep will eventually result in more points won.

"But wait," you say. "I have watched YouTube videos of professional tournaments. The pros don't always hit deep, so why should I?" I admit this is a valid point. Apparently, someone conducted a detailed analysis of YouTube videos from professional tournaments and found that 60% of serves landed in the middle portion of the court somewhere in the vicinity. So if pros do not even serve deep, why should you?

There are a couple of reasons why serve depth becomes shortened in tournament play. First, when nerves and pressure come into play, even elite pickleball players feel it and begin hitting shorter serves. No one is immune to the pressure of a tournament situation, although some players deal with it better and, in this case, serve deeper than others. The tighter the match and the bigger the moment, the more nerves come into play. Second, shorter serve depth is a holdout from conventional, outdated pickleball wisdom. Under this philosophy, points are won at the net, not the serve, so one should simply keep the ball in play. No doubt, this is how pickleball *was* historically played. However, there is room for improvement at every level of the game, from professional to recreational play. As better athletes train more exclusively to earn a living from pickleball, the average speed and depth of serves will improve. I see it happening already. Be aware of service depth and attempt to hit even a little deeper than before, especially in recreational play, to become comfortable and gain muscle memory. Again, if you win more points than you lose, you have acquired an advantage in the risk/reward paradigm.

Now that we have established depth as the operative word, where should you aim? "Serve to the backhand" is typical strategic advice, but is that enough? Before diving into this topic, let me add a caveat. If you cannot consistently serve deep yet, focus exclusively on service depth before attempting placement. Master depth before moving on to the more difficult step of depth plus placement. Overthinking is a primary cause of stupid mistakes or loss of confidence when serving, so master the first step of attaining depth before progressing to the next step.

Rather than simply serving to the backhand side, try to first identify the weaker side of the returning player. Most players' backhand side is more vulnerable, but now always. You could just as easily target the opponent's body. Aiming toward the body forces them to choose a side, making them move while returning and often making them move sideways rather than forward. This makes them uncomfortable and unstable, leading to mistakes. In addition, after hitting several serves to the same place, the opponent will likely expect the next serve in the same location. As a surprise tactic, mix up the service placement once in a while to prevent the opponents from becoming overly comfortable. When serving, attempt to make the opponent move at least one step in either direction, as hitting any shot while moving is more complex than hitting from a stable position. The more accurate and effective the serve becomes, the more you can pinpoint the opponent's weakness and pinpoint specific spots on the court to aim.

Server Positioning

Most players walk up to the line and serve without giving much thought to their own positioning. But positioning adds another strategic element that can become an advantage for your team. A couple of factors affect positioning, so let's discuss them here.

First, think ahead to the next shot. What does this mean? Most players have a stronger side when hitting the third shot (forehand or backhand), even if they are not consciously aware of it. Consider your own third shot. Which side feels more consistent or comfortable? Which side is more accurate from a deep return vs. a short return? Take advantage of this preference by hitting third shots primarily with your stronger side. If this shot yields a higher success rate, why not take advantage of it rather than letting your opponent pick on the weaker side? Become proactive by taking the third shot with your stronger side rather than simply reacting to where the opponent hits the ball. This alone will separate you from players who do not think strategically.

To make this happen when serving, stand, so the return of

serve naturally comes to your preferred side most of the time. For example, right-handed players who want to hit a backhand third shot should move from the middle of the court over a step or two towards the right when serving. Most returns would then automatically arrive toward the backhand side. Just by standing to take advantage of a preference, your third shot success rate will increase, translating to more points won. If the opponents notice this preference and attempt to avoid your strong side, you will force them to aim for a smaller area, increasing their errors. You have effectively forced them to take more risks simply by proactively standing in a particular position and thinking one shot ahead.

Second, consider the opponent's weaker returning side. Forcing them to return with their more vulnerable side raises the likelihood of errors and short returns. For example, when serving from the odd (left) side and forcing a right-handed opponent to hit a backhand return, stand toward the left side of the court to take advantage of the wide crosscourt angle. Hitting deep towards the body can also prove an effective tactic, forcing them to move one way, making them uncomfortable, and opening up the court.

The advice to stand to take advantage of an opponent's weaker return side might seem contrary to the advice about standing to take advantage of your own strength. First, remember that these are not mutually exclusive. You can serve from a position to take advantage of an opponent's weakness, then move to hit your preferred third shot. If you cannot move this quickly, consider the more important factor.

Is it more important to make the opponent hit the shot they dislike or to hit the third shot you prefer? It depends on the opponent and the situation, your strengths, and their weaknesses. At least be aware of these strategic factors, playing to your strengths and their weaknesses as much as possible.

The third aspect of positioning regards how far to step into the court. After serving or watching their partner serve, many players take a step into the court, positioning themselves a step or two in front of the baseline. This occurs from habit, the expectation of a short return, or simple carelessness. Seeing you step forward, the opponents often take advantage by placing the return deep. This drives you away from your goal of reaching the NVZ line and causes you to step back while hitting, making the third shot even more challenging. We will discuss the importance of stepping into the third shot later. For now, know that it is always preferable to step forward into the ball and towards the NVZ line when hitting the third shot. Instead of standing too far ahead, after serving or watching your partner serve, stay behind the baseline to wait for the return. I typically stand even further back, around one large step behind the baseline. This allows you to continually step into the third shot and, counter-intuitively, reach the NVZ line faster because of the increased forward momentum. Remember that an object in motion tends to stay in motion, so start back but move forward through the third shot to reach the line faster. This likely means you need to start a little further back than you are accustomed to doing.

Stacking

Stacking is just a way to take advantage of each player's preferred positioning at the NVZ line. In mixed doubles, a right-handed male player typically takes the court's odd (left) side, especially if they are the stronger, more aggressive player. This positions their forehand in the middle and makes it easier to poach. When playing with a left-handed partner (mixed doubles or not), players typically stack to ensure both players' forehands remain in the middle. However, it is essential to note that these are not hard and fast rules. If something is not working, change it. If something is working, even if unconventional, keep doing it. For example, no law states that the female player must keep her backhand in the middle. Just know that stacking is a valuable tool to take advantage of strengths and change strategies. The more your pickleball game improves, the more you will understand preferences/weaknesses and utilize stacking to take advantage of them.

Another strategy regarding stacking is to allow the person hitting the most balls to choose their comfortable side. This is especially effective for doubles games where one player is clearly targeted. The reasoning goes, the weaker player being targeted needs to feel comfortable since they hit most of the balls. In this case, rather than stacking to emphasize the better player's strength, stack to reduce the weaker player's weaknesses. Too many teams never realize this, stacking for the benefit of the stronger player rather than the weaker player. This does not always mean the female partner in mixed doubles. I have seen the guy get picked on many times. If you are the stronger player, however, be willing to give up the preferred side for the sake of your team. Sometimes this is a hard pill to swallow for aggressive mixed doubles players... like my dad...

The best way to learn about stacking is to watch YouTube videos, try it for yourself or become a certified referee. First, I recommend watching a YouTube video on stacking. Search Pickleball 411 - Stacking or click the link https://www.youtube.com/watch?v=Cqxdnr6rdfc. Stacking when serving is relatively simple compared to stacking when returning, so perhaps start by just stacking when your team is serving before moving to something more complicated. This is called a half stack because you only stack in half of the potential situations (i.e., only when serving).

Partner Communication

After serving, it is just as likely that the return will be hit to your partner, especially if the opponents consider them the weaker player. But before you serve, make sure both partners understand positioning strategy by frequently communicating, especially regarding who will hit the third shot if the ball lands in the middle of the court. This means both players need to position themselves to take advantage of their particular third shot preferences.

Again, become more proactive by deciding beforehand who takes the shot in the center and discussing which side each partner prefers. I go so far as to discuss exactly how far over I will come over the line to hit the third shot on my partner's side of the court, depending on their ability, confidence level, preferences, etc. However, remember that this must be communicated before stepping on the court or hitting the serve to avoid confusion.

Another tendency is for a non-serving partner to absentmindedly or eagerly take a step or two forward. Instantly, they become a target for the returning team. We call this person a pickleball creep. Do not become a creep! When your partner does this, kindly remind them not to creep. Before serving, visually confirm that your partner is ready behind the baseline. If the service motion takes you a step into the court, step back quickly with a split step to prepare for the return. Minor adjustments like these can make significant differences and provide valuable strategic advantages, especially in tournament situations.

Forehand vs. Backhand

Employing both backhand and forehand serves can be a good strategy for not letting the opponents become too comfortable. However, perfect a consistent forehand serve first before attempting the more difficult backhand serve. Overthinking, rushing, or trying too tricky a shot introduces inconsistency, so keep it simple and have a reliable forehand serve before adding complexity.

If interested in a backhand serve, check out "How to Hit a Backhand Pickleball Serve by Scott Moore" on Youtube or click the link: https://youtu.be/fnNm3UPiEQM.

Spin

Many higher-level players implement topspin into their serves. To hit topspin, swing in a low to high motion, brushing from underneath and over the ball. This is one situation in which some wrist movement is necessary. Try to keep the ball on the paddle as long as possible. Topspin makes the ball bounce higher and further, making the ball feel "heavier" to the opponents. This often causes them to step back unless they hit the ball immediately after it bounces. It also can jump higher than expected, which is called a kick. An unfamiliar bounce causes them not to hit the return cleanly, forcing an error, hesitation, or a weak return. Again, a topspin serve can be an effective tool but should only be added after mastering a more basic, deep, no-spin serve.

Another type of spin employed is the sidespin. Although the rule recently changed, making it illegal to utilize the paddle to generate spin, it is still legal to generate spin with your hand or fingers as long as the opponents can always see the ball. This is a high-level strategy, and spin should only be used after perfecting the deep serve. Practice the finger snap or the wrist flick to generate a spin that bounces sideways, catching your opponent wrong-footed.

Thinking Ahead

It is often said that high-level pickleball looks more like chess, with players thinking several shots ahead. What does this mean? It means to start thinking about utilizing the serve to open up spaces on the court. For example, maybe the opponent is positioned on the even (right) side and wants to hit a forehand, so they stand to the left. You could hit a wide serve, forcing them to move to hit the return. This leaves a significant gap in the middle of the court, and if they hit a short return, you can drive the ball down the middle. Even if they successfully move to the NVZ line, they will likely have to hit a backhand fourth shot, increasing your advantage with each strategically placed shot. The point is to think about strategy, not just in the current shot but also to anticipate what might happen next. Notice patterns and tendencies in the opponents to better predict and take advantage of them. Continue successful patterns whenever possible and change unsuccessful ones. At its core, pickleball strategy is about lasting longer than the opponents, waiting for them to make a mistake or open up a space on the court.

The Element of Surprise

Whatever serve you hit, hitting it every time leads to predictability. Once in a while, mix up serves by hitting short, wide, a lob serve, or the opponent's stronger side. Keeping the opponents guessing prevents them from becoming too comfortable. Make them supply their own power by hitting a lob serve. Or make them move while returning, as they sometimes hesitate or do not make solid contact. Don't be afraid to experiment. And remember, if something is not working, change it. If something is working, keep doing it. Better to change tactics and have a chance of winning than losing with the perfect service strategy.

Conclusion

Hitting deep is the operative word when serving. Use the large muscles and aim higher, rather than simply hitting harder to do this effectively. Try to get used to consistently hitting deep serves so that you win more points both directly and indirectly.

Chapter 4

The Return

By Daniel

In theory, like the serve, most players understand that they should generally return deeper. However, in reality, most play it safe by merely keeping the ball in play. I know this mentality well. Missing a return in pickleball stings more than missing a serve, especially at a crucial time because it is associated with losing a point. Missing a return towards the end of a game can mean the difference between winning and losing a match. I have looked back on an entire tournament in disgust, lamenting the one return I missed at 11-11 in game 3 of the finals. While recognizing this pain, I also realize that learning and hitting deeper returns provide excellent rewards over time. By understanding the reasoning, acknowledging the risk, and practicing deep returns, the return can be a weapon in your journey to becoming a better pickleball player.

First, remember that not all missed returns are created equal. A return missed in the net is much worse than a return missed deep. Why? When missing a return deep, at least you attempted the correct shot. Dialing it down just a little will result in an effective shot that makes it difficult for the opponents to score. Let's return to the risk/reward analysis. The rewards outweigh the risks if you miss one return per game out but consistently hit all other returns deep (setting up a difficult third shot for the opponents). Most opponents cannot consistently hit effective third shots from deep within their own court, setting you up for some net errors and many high drop shots that will allow you to take advantage of the fourth shot.

Here is another way to think about it. The difference between a deep return and an out (long) return is between a great shot and losing the point. The difference between a short return and missing in the net is between a mediocre return and losing the point. Since the downside in both cases is losing the point, the upside (hitting a great return) is much more significant for deep returns. Keep practicing hitting deep in recreational games to become comfortable. Eventually, muscle memory will take over. Some of those returns that sail out in recreational games will land in when nerves become more of a factor in a tournament situation.

Finally, deep returns help you take advantage of a short serve or neutralize a deep one. A short return shifts the initial advantage against your team, meaning you must fight an uphill battle for the rest of the point. You may win some rallies after hitting a short return, but the odds are against you. On the other hand, Returning deep maintains your advantage as the returning team. Since the serving team must stay back, it is imperative that the returning team hit a deep return and reach the NVZ line first, ideally before hitting the fourth shot. Changing your mentality from just getting the return in to actually setting yourself up for success throughout the entire point will give you an advantage over players who do not know how to construct a point to their advantage.

Step In

To consistently return deep, it is essential to utilize the forward momentum of your body weight. Rather than stepping or falling backward or simply swinging harder, use your body to drive the ball deeper into the opponents' court. The best way to do this is to first turn your shoulders perpendicular to the net when swinging. Make sure to take a comfortable and complete step forward as you swing from below the ball, making sure to engage the shoulders and core. Follow through to finish your swing well past the contact point. Stepping in provides more consistency and power by getting the body involved without swinging harder.

Many players tend to stand too far forward (sometimes in front of the baseline) while waiting to return. This could be out of habit, hoping to prevent a short serve, or simply thoughtlessness. Whatever the reason, a deep serve will force you to step back while hitting the return.

Two bad things happen in this scenario. First, momentum is directed away from the ball by stepping back, making a deep return more difficult. Bodyweight actively works against you when stepping back, so you must swing harder to achieve the same depth. This decreases accuracy and puts more strain on individual body parts like the arm and shoulder.

Second, because the followthrough actually takes you backward, you are now standing further away from the objective of reaching the NVZ line before the opponents. Unless your name is Usain Bolt, reaching the NVZ line before the opponents is going to be almost impossible. You must now hit the fourth shot from no man/woman's land, a much more difficult proposition fraught with perils. These include hitting the net, popping the ball up, and missing wide. All these negative results result from the preventable, lazy, or uninformed reason of standing too far forward while waiting to return serve.

The most common objection, especially by older players, to standing further back is the possibility of a short serve. You may occasionally lose a point by standing further back due to the opponents' perfectly placed or unintentional short serve. However, this is rare compared to losing the rally due to a short return. Even if the opponents attempt to serve short, they will make more mistakes as they aim close to the net and the NVZ line. You have forced them to take more risk simply by standing slightly further back. Standing one or two steps behind the baseline allows a complete step-in motion into the return of serve, with the momentum carrying you closer to the NVZ line. Stepping in this much might feel exaggerated at first, but reaching the NVZ line before the opponents is so strategically important that it's worth exaggerating this motion a little. Personally, I start even further back, 3-4 steps behind the baseline or as far as the back fence allows. I like to run towards the return, slow down as I swing, then carry on forward and reach the NVZ as fast as possible. You don't have to go to this extreme length, but remember to start far enough back so that you can step forward into every return.

Use your Preferred Side

Much like the serve, many players stand in the middle of the court when waiting to return. If the serve comes to their forehand side, they hit a forehand, and if it comes to their backhand side, they hit a backhand. This, however, means letting the opponents dictate the point. We call this reactive pickleball. Reactive pickleball means responding to what the opponents do without having a plan of your own. Our suggestion is to stop allowing your opponents to decide which shot you will hit. Instead, become proactive, choose the side you prefer to hit the return with, and use that stroke most of the time. For right-handed players who consistently hit deeper returns on the forehand side (most people's preference), take a step or two towards the left side of the court, opening up the forehand side. This makes it harder for the opponents to make you hit a backhand. If they do aim for your backhand, sometimes they will miss wide, giving away a free point. You are now baiting them, causing them to take more risks and make more mistakes. Remember, all you have to do to hit almost exclusively forehands is simply stand further over to the left while lining up for your return. If they occasionally hit a near-perfect serve and force a backhand, just do your best to return it with some loft and depth, creating time to reach the NVZ line. The return might not go as deep as a forehand, but because you rarely hit your non-preferred side, it won't typically affect the game's outcome. Also, if forced to hit your non-preferred side, remember to hit deep and down the middle so your partner can help on the next shot.

The difference in return depth between their preferred and weaker sides is massive for some players. Take advantage of every strength available by using your stronger side as much as possible. True, by standing further to one side, you might occasionally get burned with an unexpected serve to the other side. But like the short serve, losing from this scenario is not as common as losing the point by hitting a short return. So again, weigh the risks and the rewards. See if you consistently come out ahead by standing further over to open up your stronger stroke and hitting deeper returns. My guess is that you will.

Use your Entire Body

This section is similar to the service chapter, with the additional element of turning the shoulders and engaging the core. Engaging the core in this way is similar to swings in other sports such as golf or tennis. In the serve section, we said using the more stable, large muscles of the torso and legs generates more power and control than using small muscles like the wrist, arms, and shoulders independently. These smaller muscles should be used too, but only in conjunction with the larger muscles. Using your entire body allows for a relaxed, controlled, and powerful motion originating from the core.

To better utilize your legs and torso when returning serve, make sure to turn the shoulders approximately 90 degrees when preparing to hit the return. As you hit the shot facing sideways, twist from the torso back to a position of looking forward toward the net. This twisting motion generates smooth power, having engaged the strongest muscles in the body. Don't forget to use your legs. Bend the knees rather than the waist so the ball lifts effortlessly, giving greater height and depth to the return. After making the complete shoulder turn, step in as you take a full, comfortable swing. Make sure the ball is far enough away to fully extend your arm at the point of contact. Swinging from too close to the body means losing power. Watch the ball closely for as long as possible to ensure contact in the middle of the paddle. Swinging up and through, extend your arm until your shoulder is almost touching your jaw on the forehand side.

To avoid confusion, here is the exact returning sequence I remind myself to use:

1. Start further back.

2. Split step. This is a tennis term, but basically, the

moment the opponent hits the serve, get into an athletic position (knees slightly bent, shoulder-width apart) by taking a small hop or stutter step. The split step is optional but make sure you are in an athletic, ready position when the opponents serve.

3. Turn sideways. Depending on whether you hit a forehand or a backhand, you will need to turn 90 degrees clockwise or counterclockwise.

4. Step in and go from a sideways position back to facing forward as you swing all the way through the ball.

5. Run to the NVZ line as quickly as possible.

Aim Higher

Aiming higher applies as much to the return section as it did for the serve. Aim higher to raise the return depth and reduce net errors. Most players aim too low, meaning they make more net errors and the ball bounces in the middle of the opponents' court. This makes for an easier third shot and allows them to move forward to the NVZ line, setting off an adverse chain reaction discussed previously. Instead, make them hit at least a couple of shots before they earn the right to reach the NVZ line. This process begins with a deep return. Make sure you arrive at the NVZ line first by hitting a higher, deeper return. Not only will you reach the NVZ line first, but many opponents will also have difficulty hitting an effective third shot from a deep return. This means more attackable balls for your team. When returning, make sure to aim higher by swinging in a low to high motion. When the paddle face is open, the ball goes higher and deeper. This can be achieved without swinging any harder or changing the swing motion.

Compact Backswing

Many players take a large, full backswing when returning serve. As a tennis player, I understand this temptation. I was told to draw a figure 8 with the tennis racket innumerable times. Since the ball originates from so far away in pickleball, it feels like you have enough time to wind up and crush the ball with a colossal backswing. However, a giant swing doesn't necessarily help generate more power. Power comes from the core and legs rather than the arms, so the followthrough is more critical than the backswing. It is also more difficult to effectively time a large backswing, making the shot less consistent. Even slight miss-timing results in the ball flying out or into the net. This might be ok for a slow return that is easy to time perfectly, but a compact return is preferable as you move up in skill level and the returns get faster. Keep the backswing short and sweet, so the paddle's contact point is consistent, solid, and in front of the body. This is the best way to hit a deep return, even when the serve is deep.

Follow Through

Conversely, following through is extremely important. Though the backswing should be compact, the followthrough should be extended well past the contact point. To exaggerate the motion, finish the swing by extending your arm as far as it will go. Some players even swing through to the point where their shoulder touches their chin when hitting a forehand. Swinging completely through the shot ensures a consistently deep return. Whatever you do, don't hesitate or abbreviate the swing. Swing through with a fluid, constant forward motion, maintaining the same swing speed through the entire shot. In addition to better depth, swinging through keeps the ball on the paddle longer, giving you more control. Instead of a motion involving only the wrist or arms, swing entirely through with the entire body and large muscles engaged.

Placement

Where should you hit the return? This is one of the most common questions asked regarding the return of serve. We have already established that it should be hit deep, so now let's discuss precisely where on the court to aim. Most players do not give it much thought, so simply knowing where to aim can provide a strategic advantage. But first, another caveat. Like serving, master a deep return before moving onto the more difficult task of combining depth and placement. Deep is still the operative word and the most critical component of an effective return, so learn to hit consistently deep returns before moving on to picking on a particular opponent or that opponents' weaker side.

To the Weaker Player's Weaker Side

In tournament play particularly, hitting the weaker player's weaker side is often the best strategy. The more vulnerable side is typically the backhand, but again not necessarily. Many players prefer their backhand third shot drop (I know I do), so returning to their backhand may actually play into their strength. Observe which side they prefer and attempt to hit it away from their preference as much as possible without taking excessive risks. If you don't know which side they favor, hit straight to their body and see which side they choose. You will learn the answer quickly. If you don't know who they consider the weaker player, hit the middle and observe who takes the third shot. The player who does not take the ball in the middle is likely weaker, at least when hitting a drop shot. If there is no clear weaker player, it probably doesn't matter who you target, so just attempt to hit either player's more vulnerable side.

Down The Middle

One of the best strategies for reducing errors when returning (almost all shots, for that matter) is to hit down the middle. By eliminating the possibility of missing the return wide, you have reduced the possible errors by 1/3. The only other potential errors are missing in the net or missing long. You have reduced the possibility of net errors by aiming higher, effectively eliminating 2/3 of all possible mistakes. Also, by hitting down the middle, if the opponents have not identified who takes that shot, they may become confused, with both or neither players going for it. Hitting down the middle also takes away angles, reducing open spaces on your side of the court. Finally, if you are prone to hesitation, simply decide to hit down the middle beforehand to reduce the number of decisions you have to make. You have gained a strategic advantage if hitting down the middle every time reduces overall errors. The team that makes fewer mistakes almost always wins, so do whatever it takes to minimize mistakes.

Get your Partner Involved

Hitting the return crosscourt (back to the person who served) makes it difficult for your partner to get involved on the next shot. This is because your partner must cover their own line, making it difficult for them to poach. Instead, try returning down the line or down the middle to the player who did not serve. This is especially true when returning from the court's even (right) side with a right-handed partner. Hitting down the line allows your partner to poach with their forehand or make their presence known by moving towards the middle. This puts pressure on the opponents, even if your partner does not decide to poach. In their attempt to avoid the poacher, many players hit too close to the line, sometimes missing wide. Adding pressure also causes more net errors and high balls, adding to the points your team wins directly or indirectly.

I don't have any statistics to back this up, but there is another reason to return down the line to the non-serving partner. For some reason, I find that the non-serving partner is typically less prepared to hit the third shot than the serving partner. Like a left fielder not paying attention, sometimes the non-serving partner is unprepared and seems to make more mistakes. Use that to your advantage by returning to them and seeing if they are prepared.

The Non-Returning Partner

Once in a while, I'm asked, "where should I look when my partner is returning the ball?" In other words, if my partner is returning and I am already standing at the NVZ line, should I turn and watch my partner return the serve, or should I keep my eyes directed at the opponents? I'm sure there are different approaches to this question, but I like to turn and watch my partner for a couple of reasons. First, it's an excellent habit to constantly watch the ball. When the point really gets going, it's vital to keep your eyes on the ball, and this habit begins with watching the return. Second, when I watch my partner return, I know where they place the ball on my opponents' side of the court. If my partner returns down the line, it's much easier for me to take the middle and attempt to poach, or at least put pressure on them by standing in the middle of the court. If I can show my opponents' that I am willing to poach, they are more likely to avoid me, leading to mistakes. If your partner returns crosscourt, stay put to avoid being passed down the line. By basing your movement on your partner's return, you can play higher percentage pickleball and gain an advantage whenever possible.

In addition, especially when standing on the left (odd) side as the non-returning partner, communicate with your partner and let them know to return down the middle or down the line rather than cross court. This allows the non-returning partner to step over towards the middle and pressure the opponent to hit the third shot. Most players tend to avoid the non-returning partner waiting at the NVZ line, especially those poaching. It also puts the non-returning partner in a better position to poach or hit an aggressive fourth shot, preferably a volley. Often the non-returning partner can volley when the returning partner would have had to let it bounce, so returning down the line allows your team to be more aggressive. In general, non-returning partners should be aggressive unless their partner hits a short or crosscourt return. They are better positioned to hit an aggressive fourth shot than their partner because they are already waiting and in position at the NVZ line.

When Your Team is Stacking

In general, return down the line when your team is stacking. Your opponent must hit a crosscourt passing shot to beat you when you return down the line. If you return crosscourt, they can hit a much easier passing shot down the line. Remember that a down-the-line passing shot is always easier than a crosscourt one. Because you have to cover so much distance when stacking on the return side, returning down the line gives you the best chance of reaching the NVZ line without being passed. As discussed earlier, it also allows your partner a much better chance of getting involved in the point and helping you out in a pinch.

Spin and Slice

Both topspin and slice are practical tools when returning

serve. Slice, in particular, is frequently utilized when hitting a backhand return. Slice returns tend to sail deeper and stay low after bouncing. This makes it difficult for the opponents to lift the ball over the net and hit an effective third shot. With enough slice the ball can also skid, speeding up after bouncing and reaching the opponents before they are ready. This means the ball is too close to their body or behind them when they hit the shot.

Topspin presents an entirely different bounce and feel compared with slice. Though the ball bounces higher, it feels heavier than a slice shot. Topspin is challenging to master, though so perfect a flat or slice return before moving onto topspin. Topspin is produced by starting under the ball and rolling up and over it. Because pickleball paddles provide little texture or grip on the paddle face, the paddle angle must be pretty flat at the point of contact. Rolling over the ball on the followthrough is what produces topspin. Whether you choose to hit flat, slice, or topspin, find your go-to return that allows for consistently deep returns. Get this into muscle memory, and you will be able to return deep even in tight tournament situations.

Stacking

Stacking when returning is more confusing than serving and takes some time to learn. There are typically two ways to stack when returning serve. One is for the non-returning partner to stand off to the side of the NVZ. After hitting the return, the returning player runs crosscourt to the NVZ line, and the non-returning player slides over so that both players are in the position where they should play.

The other way to stack is to start in a normal returning position with the non-returning partner standing where they usually would at the NVZ line. Before the point begins, the non-returning player will sign to the returning player to either stay or go, typically with a closed first or open hand, respectively. If the stay signal is given, you will play out the point usually, just like when you are not stacking. If the go sign is given, the non-returning player will slide over to the opposite side, and the returning player will run crosscourt to the NVZ line. Once again, this can be very confusing in writing, so the best way to learn stacking is to watch a YouTube video or practice on the court.

https://www.youtube.com/watch?v=Cqxdnr6rdfc

The Return vs. the Drive

In the third shot section, we will discuss the third shot drop vs. third shot drive, breaking down the drop shot in more detail. For now, know that the return mechanics are almost identical to the drive mechanics. Stepping in, using your whole body, having a compact backswing, and swinging completely through all apply equally to the drive as they do to the return. Try to keep these two shots as similar as possible to gain muscle memory and develop consistency.

Conclusion

In conclusion, the objective of the return is essentially the same as the serve: to keep the ball deep, make it difficult for the opponents, and therefore win more points. To do this, aim higher, use forward weight transfer, aim for the middle of the court and keep the backswing small. All these things will make you a better returner.

Chapter 5

The Third Shot

By Daniel

Just mentioning the third shot elicits consternation from seasoned pickleball players and confusion from newbies. Many a player has given up on attempting it or even pickleball itself, recalling nightmares of lofting the ball too high while the opponent smacks an overhead squarely at their body. No wonder this infamous shot evokes fear, making it even more challenging to execute in the heat of the moment. However, this does not have to be the case. The third shot indeed is one of the most complex skills to master. Players sometimes talk of a dark period in their pickleball life where they survived the third shot drop learning phase, forcing themselves to practice at the expense of losing every recreational game. However, its difficulty is a barrier to entry that separates intermediate from advanced players, recreational from competitive. Rather than something to fear, learn to make it a weapon in your arsenal, giving you a competitive edge. To better develop this shot, we will discuss various aspects of it, practicing it correctly, and some doubles strategies regarding working with your partner to maximize its effectiveness.

What is it?

The third shot drop is so named because of its timing in the point. After the serve and the return, it is the third shot hit (imagine that) in the sequence of a pickleball rally. The shot is typically hit with some arc so that it ideally "drops" as it clears the net, landing hopefully somewhere in the opponents' unattackable area. When hit successfully, it allows the serving team (the third shot dropping team) to move forward and reach or at least approach the NVZ line, where they have a greater chance of success than when playing from the baseline or transition zone (also known as no-man's land). As many players know, this sequence of events does not always happen as planned. But from the perspective of the serving team, what I described is the ideal development of a point after hitting the third shot drop.

It is worth mentioning that the third shot does not necessarily need to be a drop shot, and the drop shot does not have to be hit exclusively on the third shot of a rally. There are situations when you may want to drive the third shot instead of drop, but we will discuss these scenarios in greater detail later in the chapter. For now, be aware that the third shot drop is an all-encompassing phrase. It is synonymous with a drop shot. It just so happens that it most often occurs on the third shot of the point, although you must sometimes hit a fifth shot drop or even a seventh shot drop to move all the way forward to the NVZ line.

Let's return to the USA Pickleball's definition of the drop shot and discuss some of its finer points, which are as follows.

1. The drop is a soft shot hit off a bounce from deep in the court, intended to land in the opponents' NVZ, preferably close to the net.

2. Allows the hitting team to follow the shot to the NVZ line. It is the primary third shot, allowing the serving team to approach the net after the return of serve, but it can also be effective anytime the opponents are at the net.

3. One of the more difficult shots to master.

USA Pickleball's definition includes the ball bouncing into the opponent's NVZ, preferably close to the net. I tend to disagree with this requirement for three reasons. First, trying to bounce the ball as close to the net as possible within the NVZ means sometimes hitting the ball so low that the ball catches the net, automatically losing the point for your team. As discussed, it is almost always preferable to play with a comfortable margin for error over the net. Even if the ball floats high, at least you force the opponents to work rather than giving it away by losing to the net. Second, after hitting the return of serve, many opponents cannot physically reach the NVZ line quickly or do not know they should play from the NVZ line. Hitting a short drop shot when the opponents have stayed back, or you have hit a deep serve actually allows the other team to move forward to the NVZ line easier and removes your team's advantage. You are essentially correcting their mistakes and giving them a 50/50 chance of winning the point by inviting them to move forward. A better option in this scenario is to drive the ball at the opponents' feet, keeping them back and denying them the chance to play from the NVZ line. Finally, many players tend to back away from the line, preferring to let the ball bounce rather than volleying. Hitting the drop shot as short as possible in the NVZ allows the opponents to make an easier decision to dink the next shot. Hitting the drop shot slightly deeper where the opponents have to make a split-second decision forces them to scoot back or hit a problematic volley. Both raise the likelihood of making a mistake.

A Better Definition for the Third Shot Drop

Here is my preferred definition: A shot typically hit softly by the serving team, aimed at the opponents' feet, allowing the serving team to move forward towards the NVZ line.

The main difference is that the target is their feet wherever the opponents are standing. Forcing the opponents to hit up from a low position raises the likelihood of hitting it into the net or too high, allowing your team to attack. This is a better definition because it accounts for the possibility that the opponents are not already at the NVZ line, suddenly changing the target from the NVZ line to wherever the opponents are positioned.

Third Shot Drive

You should most often hit the third shot as a drop shot since that is the most consistent, guaranteed way to move forward and neutralize your disadvantage. However, it is worth noting that pros have started implementing the third shot drive more often because an effective drive also sometimes allows the serving team to move forward. The question then becomes, "when is it smart to drive instead of drop"? Here are the four scenarios that give you a license to drive according to their frequency. It is wise to drop in other situations rather than drive the third shot.

When the return is short and high. Notice the emphasis on both short and high. When the return of serve is short but low, the ball does not bounce high enough to hit an effective drive. When the return of serve is high but deep, the opponents usually have enough time to prepare for the drive. Therefore, only hit a third shot drive when the return arrives short and high. This allows you to hit hard and down and perhaps catch the opponents off guard.

When the opponents cannot or do not move forward. We discussed this scenario briefly, but any time the opponents do not move forward to the NVZ line is an excellent time to drive the ball towards their feet. The best way to set up this scenario is by hitting a deep serve into the opponents' court. This forces them to return from behind the baseline, making it a difficult shot and requiring that they run further to reach the NVZ line. Many opponents will not reach the line in time for the subsequent fourth shot, making it much more challenging to maintain their advantage. Another scenario is when the opponents are not aware that they should move forward immediately after the return of serve. This is another time to take advantage and drive the ball deep into their court.

When the return leaves no other option. Sometimes the return of serve is so deep, fast, or low that you feel uncomfortable attempting a third shot drop. It is acceptable to occasionally drive the ball in this situation, hoping the next shot will be easier. After hitting the third shot drive, however, many players go into all-out drive mode, losing the ability or the awareness that they need to hit soft. Because the opponents are prepared and positioned at the NVZ line, these are high-risk, low reward shots. After hitting a third shot drive, hit a fifth shot drop, allowing your team to move forward to the NVZ line.

To surprise your opponents or be unpredictable. After hitting drop shots consistently, sometimes you can catch the opponents off guard with a drive. When used occasionally, this can be an effective surprise tactic. However, most pickleball players err on the side of hitting the drive too often, so only use this strategy sparingly.

In all other situations, prepare for and hit a third shot drop. Your go-to shot or autopilot should be a soft drop shot, not a hard drive. Make sure to hit the drop shot almost every time and hit a drive only when there is an apparent reason. Many players make the mistake of hitting every shot hard simply because it feels good or out of habit, not because it is an effective strategy that wins them points. Instead, ingrain the third shot drop into muscle memory, making it second nature.

The Difference between the Return and the Drive

In the previous section, we discussed the return in detail and mentioned that the mechanics of the return and the drive are similar. This section will discuss the differences between the return of serve and the drive.

The primary difference between the return and the drive is the opponents' positioning. When returning serve, the opponent returning the serve must stand near the baseline. However, the opponents are often already positioned at the NVZ line when hitting a drive. This means that hitting a high, slice drive is not an appealing option. Instead, the drive must stay lower over the net to avoid being attacked, making a flat or topspin shot the better choice. In addition, the placement of the drive must be

adjusted based on the opponents' position and skill levels. If one opponent is further back, target that person. If both opponents are positioned at the NVZ line, hitting toward the middle is often the best option unless one player is clearly weaker than the other.

How to hit the Drop Shot

There are numerous ways and techniques to hit a drop shot like every other shot. Rather than discussing all the specific stroke techniques, let's discuss some overarching tendencies, guidelines, and strategies to help you improve while developing your own unique style. Remember, whatever your style is, doing the same stroke consistently every time is the best way to improve.

Swing Through

An incomplete followthrough is the most common drop shot mistake I see. Because the third shot is typically hit softly, many players stop the paddle mid-swing, fearing hitting the ball high. This fear of the drop shot often leads to hesitation. Hesitation is deadly. When you hesitate and stop swinging midway, all ball control is lost, along with any chance of a consistent third shot drop. The solution is to slow down the swing speed but follow through completely. Follow through until your shoulder is close to your chin after swinging on the forehand side. This may feel exaggerated at first, but it will get you into the habit of following through entirely and consistently.

Swinging entirely through the ball does not mean you must swing harder. Instead, use an even, smooth, confident followthrough. Try to maintain the same swing speed through the entire shot. You might feel like you are swinging too slow at first, but that is fine. When hitting a drop shot you need less power than you think. Instead of fearing the drop shot, think about the positive outcomes of hitting a good shot. Fear, anxiety, and lack of confidence are no way to play pickleball. Practice drop shots and drill with a partner, hitting from various positions in the court to build confidence. And when playing, commit to the shot by expecting to hit the ball well. As Henry Ford said, "Whether you think you can, or you think you can't - you are usually right."

Another positive outcome of following through is that the ball stays on the paddle a split second longer, providing more control. Imagine keeping the ball on the paddle as long as possible, rather than letting it pop off immediately. This will give you much more control and better accuracy.

Weight Transfer

Always step into the ball, moving forward and not away from the ball while swinging. Here is a scenario that might sound familiar. Your partner (it's always their fault, right) serves and takes two steps forward into the court, waiting to hit the third shot. The returning team sees this and powers a return deep towards them. The ball lands close to your partner's feet, forcing them to take a step back while simultaneously attempting to hit a drop shot. Off-balance and stepping back, they loft the ball high, and the opponent promptly smashes it at you, branding a pickleball mark into your skin for the day. Your partner might apologize, or they may even blame you, saying, "why didn't you get that?" Either way, you have lost the point, primarily because they stood too far forward while waiting to return. I see this scenario ad nauseam, even at the pro level. This person is a pickleball creeper, a player who creeps forward when they should stand further back to wait for the return. When you see this scenario unfold, you have our permission to politely remind them not to be a creep.

Starting further back does two positive things. First, you can step forward into the third shot, gaining momentum moving forward into the ball rather than away from it. This means that you don't have to swing as hard to achieve the same amount of power while still maintaining control of the ball. If you have trouble getting enough power to clear the net, just try stepping into the ball more. Second, stepping in helps you reach the NVZ line faster. The followthrough takes you one step closer to the line when stepping into the third shot. The followthrough takes you one step away when stepping back or away from the net. You then have to stop, start your momentum moving forward, then get stopped again by the next shot, making it more difficult to reach the NVZ line. Taking longer to reach the NVZ line usually means hitting at least one additional shot from the transition zone, lowering the probability of your team reaching the NVZ line and winning the point.

Lifting

Unfortunately for all of us, gravity never stops working. Specifically for the third shot drop, this means hitting the ball from low to high to lift it up and over the net. Many players stand straight with no bend in their knees, attempting to hit the third shot drop with little to no arc. That works if you hit a perfect shot that barely skims the net. Unfortunately, more often than not, the ball either hits the net or sails too high, directly into the opponents' strike zone. Remember, it is called a drop shot because it is supposed to actually drop as it gets to the opponents.

A better technique is to bend your knees so that you can scoop or lift the ball from underneath. Attempt to clear the net by around 1-3 feet. With an arc, the apex could be as high as six feet over the net, so the ball drops when it reaches the opponent. The opponents should have to hit upon the next shot, whether they volley or dink. Whatever you do, make sure the ball falls as it reaches the opponents. If the ball rises as it reaches them, it is attackable, so prepare for a difficult fifth shot. Even if the ball sometimes goes too high, give yourself plenty of margin for error so that you do not take yourself out of the point. Make your opponents beat you!

Footwork

I cannot emphasize enough the importance of moving your feet. So many players plant their feet like they are stuck in wet cement while waiting to hit the next ball. If a gust of wind blows, the ball is hit with spin, or it takes an unexpected bounce, the ball can quickly move too close or too far away from your body to hit from a balanced position. Neither of these leads to consistent, unattackable drop shots. Instead, make minor adjustments with your feet while the ball travels toward you, staying on your toes. The key is to start moving early, as soon as the opponent hits the ball, and take frequent small steps rather than lunging or waiting. This allows you to hit the drop shot from a balanced position, even if the ball doesn't arrive precisely where you anticipated.

Many players start moving after the ball bounces on their side. This is far too late. As you prepare for the third shot, start moving your feet as soon as the opponent makes contact with the ball. Aim to arrive well before the ball does to the spot from where you will hit the third shot. Get your body into position so that you can hit every drop shot from the same balanced, comfortable place. Too many players hit one shot with their arm fully extended, the next shot jammed close to their body, the next off their back foot, etc. That is not a formula for consistency. Whatever swing you have, it should look the same every time. This means you must move your feet early to get your body into a ready position, allowing you to hit from the most comfortable, balanced, and consistent position.

Margin of error

Many players simply aim their drop shots too close to the net. This is great when successful, but your team immediately loses the point if the shot is even slightly low. Remember, most players are beaten by the net more than their opponents. Give the opponents more opportunities to beat you because most opponents cannot do it. My strategy is to hit even higher over the net at the beginning of a game or tournament when I'm nervous, not thoroughly warmed up, or when the opponents hit a challenging return. That way, I make sure I am not giving away free points, even if I allow my opponents to attack some balls. When the return is short or when I feel dialed in, I aim slightly lower because I feel more confident.

Topspin or Slice?

Many players watch pros hitting with topspin or slice and learn to emulate them. My response is the same with any shot: learn to hit consistently without anything flashy before adding more complex shots. At every level, simply being more consistent is enough to win most of the time. Only at the most advanced and professional levels do you actually need to make things happen and actively force your opponents to make mistakes. Even at the higher intermediate levels, opponents will usually make mistakes for you and beat themselves if you can become more consistent. So master the basics before moving on to more complicated techniques like spin.

If you are ready to learn some additional drop shot skills, here are my thoughts. When the return is deep or fast, I hit a slice backhand. For me, the backhand slice is a more consistent, reliable drop shot to help me get out of trouble. I can't attack with the backhand, but I know I can consistently get the ball in play. Instead, I hit my forehand when the return looks easier, shorter, or bounces higher. It's less consistent, but I can hit it harder and use topspin, making it more aggressive and harder to handle. This way, I put pressure on my opponents when they hit a poor return but don't give away free points when they hit a great one.

Using Your Body

I often see players using the arm or wrist independently of the rest of their body when hitting drop shots. Instead, think about using your whole body, not just independent parts. As discussed earlier, weight transfer helps with power, so use your entire body to slow down the swing. For example, when utilizing slice, swing through with the whole arm rather than chopping down with the wrist. As a general rule, the larger the muscles you engage while swinging, the stronger and more consistent your shots will be. This will help you become a better, more consistent, and accurate player.

Where

Now we are getting into the nitty-gritty of the drop shot and the strategy behind it. When thinking about where to hit the drop shot, there are four primary locations that I recommend, listed here in order of importance:

1. To the player who hit the return of serve

2. To the weaker player

3. To the weaker side, typically the backhand

4. To open spaces on the court

Let's break each of those down:.

The player who hit the return. When setting up for doubles, the non-returning partner on the returning team stands at the NVZ line at the beginning of the point. This means that the player who hits the return must run as quickly as possible to the NVZ line to join their teammate. The average age of a pickleball player in America is close to 60, and their 40-yard dash time is not getting any faster. Many players cannot reach the NVZ line before the third shot reaches them, catching them out of position (especially after a deep serve). Aiming for the player who hit the return of serve allows you to gain the advantage by making them hit the fourth shot before they are ready or preferably before they even reach the NVZ line. Even if they reach the NVZ line successfully, they may be unbalanced, moving, or unprepared for the next shot, potentially missing or hitting a shot that you can take advantage of.

The weaker player. In tournament play, aiming for the weaker player is a common strategy. Even if the weaker player is already positioned at the NVZ line, aiming for them can be effective if they make more mistakes or hit shots that are easier to handle. Hitting towards the weaker player takes the pressure off, as you no longer need to hit a perfect shot. They are less likely to make you pay for a poor drop shot, so hitting towards them feels more comfortable. It isolates the weaker player by taking the stronger player out of the point.

Note: This is not a strategy we recommend for recreational play. The purpose of recreational play is to improve, not just to win. When playing a recreational game, hit mainly to the person who returned serve to hit the correct shot, not pick on a particular player. Playing the right shot and perhaps even targeting the stronger player allows for faster improvement in your own game. Stop worrying about winning a dumb recreational match. Instead, use those games to improve and prepare for tournament play. I always know if someone is interested in improving or just winning by how many balls they hit me. Those who just care about winning avoid me like the plague and thereby lose out on an excellent opportunity to improve. Coincidentally, they are also usually the players bragging to their friends about "taking x number of points off me" even though they didn't hit a single ball in my direction.

The weaker side. Most players' backhands are more vulnerable than their forehands. Playing to the weaker side, particularly in the middle of the court, is a good strategy for setting up the point. I want to elaborate briefly on hitting towards the middle of the court. When the weaker side is along the sideline, and you aim too close to the line, sometimes you will miss wide, automatically losing the point. When the weaker side is in the middle of the court, it is very difficult to miss wide, eliminating one of three possible errors (long, wide and low). Hit the drop shot to the opponent's weaker side in the middle of the court to reduce errors and gain some free points. Just like aiming a little higher over the net, play with a margin of error on the sidelines to reduce free point giveaways. This alone will make the difference between winning and losing some matches.

To open spaces on the court. Sometimes teammates leave a large gap or stand too close together, opening up large sections of the court. Hitting into open spaces is a good strategy because when the opponents have to move to retrieve the ball, they are more likely to make an error. When they move for the ball, they often cannot return to their original position in time, opening spaces on the court to exploit. Pickleball is about moving opponents, creating spaces, and hitting vacated spaces. This is especially true of dinking, but the process often begins as early as the drop shot.

Moving Forward

Now let's talk about what to do after hitting the third shot, both when it's successful and unsuccessful. First, we will define a successful drop shot as one that the opponents cannot attack and an unsuccessful drop shot as one that they can attack. We will also define four scenarios and discuss what to do in each situation. The four scenarios are: 1) After hitting a successful drop shot. 2) After hitting a drop shot that is too high and therefore attackable. 3) After hitting a drive from an aggressive position. 4) After hitting a drive from a defensive position. Most third shots fall into one of these four categories, so we will discuss each of them in further detail. After that, we will discuss what to do as the partner of the person hitting the third shot, where to stand, when to move forward, etc.

When the drop shot is successful. The reason to hit a drop shot is to move forward and play from the NVZ line. After hitting a successful low drop shot, you should move forward. Ideally, you move forward to the NVZ line but if you cannot make it all the way, proceed as far as possible until the opponent strikes the ball. The moment they make contact, do a split step so that you are completely stopped, facing the opponent hitting the ball, with your knees slightly bent. Too many players hit a good drop shot and admire their shot without moving forward. They don't expect the shot to be successful, don't know that they should move forward, or can't overcome their backward momentum from stepping back while swinging. Instead, always follow a successful drop shot with at least a couple of steps towards the NVZ line where you want to play pickleball.

When the drop shot is high. I'm sure you never do this, but sometimes the drop shot goes too high, allowing the opponents to hit aggressively. Running straight to the NVZ line when the opponents are attacking is a high-risk, low reward behavior that will eventually get you a pickleball tattoo. Too many players think they need to move forward at all costs or reach the NVZ line after only one drop shot. Instead, when you or your partner hit a drop shot high, stop where you are and prepare for the next shot. I try to move forward, even if it's just one small step to get me just a little closer to the line. But staying where you are and holding your ground is also acceptable.

The main thing is that you don't keep moving forward, but you also don't retreat. You may never make it to the NVZ line if you start retreating. Besides, it is tough to hit an accurate shot while moving backward. Many players give up or run away when they see a high drop shot, but with only 10 feet to cover (your half of the court), you can retrieve more aggressive shots than you think. The shot after an unsuccessful drop is called a reset and will be discussed in another section. For now, know that you should never give up on the point just because you hit one bad shot. There are plenty of transitions between defense and offense at the pro level in a single point. If you have time to panic, you have time to prepare. Get ready for the next shot and even if the ball keeps going too high, at least make your opponents beat you by making them hit one more ball.

The aggressive drive. This happens when the opponents hit the return short and high or are far from the NVZ line. In either scenario, move forward after hitting the drive. If they have stayed back, moving forward after an aggressive drive allows you to reach the NVZ line before them and often forces them back. When driving the ball after a short and high return, they usually cannot handle the speed or float the next ball too high, allowing you to attack again. In either situation, move forward after the aggressive drive to press the advantage.

The defensive drive. This is when the opponents hit a deep, hard, low, or aggressive return, and you feel uncomfortable attempting a drop shot. After hitting a drive in this scenario, just take a couple of steps forward before preparing for the next shot. The opponents will likely volley the ball at your feet. Be prepared to hit a drop shot next. Many players make the mistake of staying in drive mode and continuously driving the ball on the fifth shot, seventh shot, etc. However, becoming a better player entails the decision-making skills of knowing when to hit a drive and when to hit a drop shot and switching seamlessly between hard and soft.

What to do as the non-third shot partner

Many people ask what they should do when the return of serve is hit to their partner. For example, should they move ahead of their partner or stay parallel, seeing where the ball goes before moving forward? Typically, we say that the answer to this question depends on two main factors: How deep is the return of serve, and how skillful is your partner at hitting effective third shots?

First, when the opponent hits a deep or aggressive return, it lowers your partner's likelihood of hitting a successful third shot. In that case, stay just one or two steps ahead of your partner. Observe their shot before committing to moving any further forward. Remember that retreat is difficult, so it's better not to move too far forward before you know the quality of your partner's drop shot. If your partner hits a successful drop shot, move forward as quickly as possible, hopefully making it all the way to the NVZ line before the opponents hit the ball. Being a couple of steps ahead of your partner helps you reach the line first. Moving forward after a successful drop shot puts pressure on the opponents because they see you and know that they cannot hit the ball too high. Some will try to avoid you, missing wide.

If your partner hits a drop shot that sails high, stay where you are and prepare for the attack by stopping and preparing in an athletic position. The goal is to hit a reset shot low and get back in the point. We will discuss the reset shot in a subsequent section, but know it is difficult. It may take two or three attempts before placing a ball at the opponent's feet. As soon as this happens, move forward and play the rest of the point from the NVZ line.

In contrast, a short return raises the likelihood that your partner will hit a successful third shot. If the return is short and high, they may hit a drive. If the return is short and low, they should hit a drop shot. Either way, move forward a few steps ahead of your partner, reaching the NVZ line before the opponents hit their next shot. This is advantageous because you can attack or poach if the opponents hit too high.

Additionally, being at the line puts pressure on the opponents because they try to keep the ball low and away from you. This pressure alone can cause them to make a mistake. It also protects against a short dink hit to your partner's side, as you will be there to cover that shot. Even if you don't make it all the way to the NVZ line when your partner is hitting a drop shot, staying a couple of steps ahead helps prevent the short dink that your partner cannot cover.

One last point is where to run forward when moving in ahead of your partner. Conventional wisdom says to move straight forward to cover your half of the court. However, a better strategy is adjusting by moving towards where the third shot is headed. Cover the line if the ball goes to the person directly across from you, but cover the middle if the ball is crosscourt. By doing this, your team always protects the center, takes away angles, and prevents any spaces from opening on the court.

Second and perhaps even more critical in determining when to move ahead of your partner is this: How good are they? If they have not hit a successful third shot all day, it's probably wise to stay only a step or two ahead of them, lest you become a human sacrifice. The goal is to win the point, not to reach the line with a new tattoo, so stay back when your partner is struggling or not skillful enough to hit an effective third shot. On the other hand, if your partner consistently hits effective third shots from anywhere on the court, move ahead of them even if the return of serve is a little deeper or more aggressive. Again, it depends on your partner and how consistently they can hit third shots. No one is perfect but play the percentages to determine whether to move forward ahead of them.

Conclusion

The third shot is an essential part of any pickleball player's game since most rallies continue until at least the third shot. Practice is vital, developing muscle memory and the confidence to execute the shot effectively and consistently. Hopefully, these strategies and tips will help you improve as a player and provide new perspectives you may not have previously considered.

Chapter 6

The Volley

By Daniel

Along with the third shot, the volley is perhaps the shot that causes the most anxiety for budding pickleball players. The high stakes of even a slight mistake and the immediacy of the punishment that follows cause many players instinctively to retreat from the NVZ line, hoping to hit as few volleys as possible. Reminders of past mistakes (you or your partner's) and being hit by the subsequent smash do nothing to alleviate these concerns. Many players' sense of hesitancy when volleying is almost palpable. But there is good news. You need not live in fear. Learning to keep the ball low when volleying can be practiced and improved like any other skill. And staying near the NVZ line or returning to the NVZ line after retreating is something you can learn and improve with practice. Volleying near the NVZ line takes precious time away from opponents, putting more pressure on them. As a result of developing this skill and remaining forward, you will have more time, and your opponents will have less, meaning they will start making the mistakes instead. Knowing an opponent's tendency to retreat means you can start using that to your advantage, continuously pressuring them, aiming balls at their feet, forcing them to play from difficult positions, or keeping them off balance. Volleys are used in almost every rally, and it is essential to understand the critical elements of this shot.

Definition

A volley is any ball hit out of the air instead of allowing the ball to bounce. A volley is not necessarily hit from the NVZ line; it can happen anywhere on the court. However, the NVZ line is the most common position to volley and the most strategic. As a result, most of this chapter focuses on volleying from the NVZ line. That is not to say all volleys from the NVZ line are created equal. The situation might necessitate a backhand or a forehand volley, a swinging or a blocking volley, a low volley, or a high volley. Learning to recognize the situation and adapt the volley accordingly is crucial in developing as a pickleball player.

Ready Position

Let's begin our volleying discussion by talking about what should happen before the ball is even on your side of the court. Ready position, not reflexes, is the most essential component in volleying reaction time. Old eyes or sore muscles are often used as excuses for poor reflexes, but this argument doesn't seem to hold water. To quote "The Sports Gene" by David Epstein,

"For four decades, scientists have been constructing a picture of how elite athletes intercept speeding objects. The intuitive explanation is that the Albert Pujolses and Roger Federers of the world simply have the genetic gift of quicker reflexes that give them more time to react to the ball. Except, that isn't true. When people are tested for their "simple reaction time" - how fast they can hit a button in response to light - most of us, whether we are teachers, lawyers, or pro athletes, take around 200 milliseconds, or one-fifth of a second".

This is both good and bad news. The good news is with proper preparation and anticipation, you will have the same reaction time as anyone else. The bad news is you no longer have an excuse for poor preparation.

Let's return to the ready position, or how exactly you should hold the paddle and prepare when the ball is still on the opponents' side of the court. First, let me remind you that when the opponent contacts the ball, you do not know if the next ball will be hit soft or hard, high or low, so you must prepare for all the possibilities. Many players make the mistake of assuming that the next shot will be soft because the last shot was soft etc. The problem arises when their assumption is incorrect and they are unprepared for the next shot. Let me distinguish assumption from anticipation here. Assumption means guessing at the expense of preparation. Anticipation still involves guessing but not sacrificing any preparation.

Next, the proper paddle-ready position is a hotly debated topic, with coaches and players alike all advocating their preferred position. I tend to believe there is a range of acceptable ready positions. Depending on your play style and what shot the opponent hits, anywhere within that range may be correct. We will discuss this further in the next section.

Favoring the Backhand

What exactly does a range of acceptable ready positions mean? First, hold your paddle straight in front of your body with the tip pointing towards the opponents. Make sure your arm is extended or slightly bent at the elbow with the paddle head pointed slightly upwards. We will call this ready position 12 O'clock since the paddle is pointed directly in front of you. From this position, you can easily hit a forehand or backhand. Next, turn the paddle to the backhand side so the paddle face is rotated 90 degrees from the 12 O'clock position and the paddle face (instead of the tip) is pointing towards the opponents. We will call this position 9 O'clock (3 O'clock if you are left-handed). For most players, the ready position should be somewhere between 9 and 12 O'clock. Always keep the paddle in front of the body and point it either straight forward or slightly favor the backhand side.

Why favor the backhand side? To demonstrate, bring the paddle to the 9 O'clock position (3 O'clock if you are left-handed). Imagine first that a ball comes to your backhand side. This shot is easy because the paddle is already in the backhand position. Now a ball comes directly towards your body. You can also easily handle this shot by hitting a backhand. Finally, imagine a ball going towards your forehand side. Without flipping the paddle over to the forehand, try taking it as a backhand. It is more difficult but still possible to hit a backhand almost anywhere the ball is. It is essential to know that in a pinch or rapid-fire volley exchange, even a ball hit far to the forehand side can be taken as a backhand if you don't have time to switch the paddle over.

In contrast, ready the paddle on the forehand side at 3 O'clock (9 O'clock if you are left-handed). Imagine first that a ball comes to your forehand side. This shot is comfortable because you are already in the forehand position. Next, a ball comes towards your body. It's still possible to hit this shot but feels cramped and often involves having to move your body out of the way to avoid becoming "chicken winged." Finally, a ball is hit to your backhand side. It is virtually impossible to hit this shot as a forehand without moving significantly, which takes too long in a fast volley exchange. Unlike the backhand mechanics, the forehand does not permit a wide range of motion. The ready position should favor the backhand side for the broader range of motion, reducing your reaction time by allowing you to hit the shot with the smallest amount of effort and movement.

Adjusting to the Situation

There are an almost endless variety of situations where you could find yourself volleying. However, to simplify things, let's break down 3 common scenarios at the NVZ line: defensive, neutral, and offensive modes. Defensive mode is when you are being pushed back, forced to move, out of position, in trouble, or pressured/uncomfortable, or your opponents are hitting down on the ball. Neutral mode is when neither team has a clear advantage. Finally, offensive mode is when your opponents are pushed back, forced to move, in trouble, pressured/uncomfortable, or when you are hitting down on the ball. Simply being aware of the situation and changing the paddle's ready position can improve reaction time considerably.

As a rule of thumb, in defensive mode, favor the backhand side, bringing the paddle closer to the 9 O'clock position (3 O'clock if you are left-handed). You no longer have time to decide between hitting a forehand or a backhand, especially if the opponents are attacking. Favoring the backhand side provides the best chance of retrieving the ball and keeping the point alive. In defensive mode, picture a hockey goalkeeper, just trying not to let the puck fly past them. Another way to describe defensive mode is survival. Don't attempt too much when trying to survive; you already have enough on your hands. Get back into the point by keeping the ball soft and low. That should be the only focus. Do not hit hard or go directly from defensive to offensive without passing through neutral. Attempting to go into offensive mode too quickly raises the likelihood of errors, so get back to neutral first.

In neutral mode, there is a broader range of acceptable ready positions. Generally, the ready position in neutral mode should be closer to 12' O'clock than in defensive mode. Most players still favor the backhand side because of the broader range of motion, but not as heavily as defensive mode. Don't favor the backhand side so much that you cannot hit a forehand. Neutral mode can be tricky because you have to be ready for anything. The situation can change instantly, and you could go from neutral into offensive or defensive, hit a forehand or a backhand on the next shot. Be ready for anything and constantly expect the ball to come hard at you so that you are never caught unprepared.

Hold the paddle at or near a 12 O'Clock position in offensive mode. Most players' forehands are stronger than their backhands, so attacking with the forehand side is preferable. This could mean moving your body to take advantage of your stronger forehand side, so be prepared by staying light on your feet. Do not get stuck in cement. Keep the pressure on the opponents when in offensive mode by hitting aggressively and low toward their feet if possible or towards open spaces to keep them moving and uncomfortable. Try to stay in offensive mode by keeping the pressure on the opponents by whatever means necessary. The goal of defensive mode is to reach neutral mode, the purpose of neutral mode is to get to offensive mode, and the goal of offensive mode is to finish the point in offensive mode, preferably by forcing your opponents to make a mistake.

Grip and Power

Let's start with the grip. Many players simply grip the paddle too hard. I am not sure whether this is a habit or stress from worrying about the next ball flying at their face. A key to volleying successfully, especially in defensive or neutral mode, is softening the grip. Pretend the ball is an egg you don't want to break. Swinging too hard will crack the egg, so be gentle. When in an offensive position, smash that egg! Don't let it come back to your side. You can grip the paddle harder accordingly. That does not mean grip and swing with 100% power every time. Swing at 80% if that suffices to win the point, as swinging harder reduces consistency and increases the chances of injury. Hitting to the opponent's feet is more important than the speed of the ball, so hit with the amount of power needed to keep the ball low.

Besides grip pressure, there is the question of how to actually hold the paddle. Once again, there are multiple acceptable answers, and my advice is to find what feels comfortable. Use a prior sports background if you have one to help determine this. Tennis players tend to prefer a continental grip. To do this, hold the paddle vertically in front of you, pointing it towards your opponents. Grip the paddle so that the V between your thumb and index finger is on top. This allows for a forehand or backhand, volley or dink without changing grips. Table tennis players tend to put the index finger on the paddle face, providing better stability but less power or reach. Badminton players grip the paddle lower down the butt, enabling more wrist action. These are just examples. The point is that you should incorporate elements of any sports background into your pickleball game whenever it provides an advantage. This applies not only to the grip but to all aspects of the game. Try to keep the good habits from previous sports and eliminate the bad habits. All of us have these good and bad habits so make sure to utilize what you can and try to eliminate what you need to. Glen Peterson's video on continental, Eastern, and Western grips is a helpful visual demonstration for further information on gripping the paddle.

https://www.youtube.com/watch?v=8OHu0gRZf2o

This is an advanced technique, but some players change grips slightly depending upon the shot. For example, when hitting a serve, returning, or driving the ball, you may want to grip the paddle further down the butt to gain reach, whip, and power. Conversely, when hitting a dink, volley, or reset shot, you may want to choke up and grip closer to the paddle head for maximum control because you don't need power. Whichever grip you choose, make sure it is comfortable and that you always stick with it for that particular shot to gain consistency. If changing grips leads to inconsistency or hesitation, use the same grip for all shots. Again, this is an advanced technique that not even most pros utilize, so make sure to master one grip before experimenting with changing grips on different shots.

Paddle Angle

Like being aware of the situation (defensive, neutral offensive), you must adjust the paddle angle according to the height of the ball. The lower the ball, the greater the upward-facing or open-faced paddle should be. Please note this does not mean swinging harder. Swinging harder when the ball is low means hitting the ball into the opponents' strike zone. Conversely, the higher the contact point, the more downward-facing or close-faced the paddle must be. Practicing volleys of varying heights helps you gain a feel for changing the paddle angle quickly and effortlessly. The goal is to do it naturally without having to think, in other words, from muscle memory. Remember, the primary target when volleying is the opponents' feet. This even holds true when attacking because a smash hit to the feet is much more complicated to retrieve than one hit at body height. Making slight adjustments to the paddle angle depending on the height of the ball is a crucial skill for developing as a pickleball player. If a ball goes out or into the net, notice the paddle angle and adjust accordingly to avoid making the same mistake next time.

Everything in Front

Hit volleys in front of the body with your arm fully extended or slightly bent at the elbow. Volleying in front is critical for several reasons. First, volleying at the highest contact point possible allows you to hit down towards your opponents' feet. Letting the ball drop by waiting for it to reach your body makes it more difficult to clear the net and hit down to the opponents' feet. Finally, taking the ball earlier and higher means a better margin for error and fewer mistakes.

Second, hitting the ball in front reduces the opponents' reaction time. Hitting the ball sooner means the ball returns to their side faster, leaving them with less time to react. This causes discomfort and pressure and, therefore, errors. Notice the difference between opponents who take the ball in front and those who take it further back. Their contact point affects the amount of time you have to prepare, making you feel pressured or relaxed. Make the opponents uncomfortable by stripping as much time away as possible. And remember to follow the golden rule of pickleball: do unto others before they do unto you.

Finally, keeping the ball in front prevents the infamous chicken wing. The chicken wing happens when you get jammed trying to hit a forehand close to the body, usually around the right shoulder for right-handed players. Contacting the ball in front reduces the area and probability of getting jammed, making it harder for the opponents to exploit this weakness. Contrarily, notice when an opponent hits further back and take advantage of their forehand side near the body. As you can see, volleying in front is desirable for various reasons. Make sure you are aware of this and keep practicing it, noticing the difference between hitting in front and when you pull the paddle back out of habit.

The Backswing

Many players take too large of a backswing when volleying. Especially when the ball starts going faster, there is no time for a large backswing. After taking a large backswing, the next ball often returns before finishing the last swing. Remember the advice in previous sections to keep the ball in front of your body. Swing with a crisp, compact and concise motion that allows clean contact and a swift recovery to the ready position if the opponent hits the ball back to you.

A large backswing is justified (though not always necessary) when attacking a high, floating ball. In this case, you have permission to take a large backswing since there is time, and the next ball will not likely come back aggressively. In this scenario, use the core to achieve power rather than the arms alone. Taking exaggerated swings can injure your shoulder, so use the whole body to avoid straining a single part. There is the added benefit of keeping the swing shorter while retaining the ability to generate power.

Follow Through

Like the paddle angle, the follow-through constantly changes depending on the situation. The block volley (defensive) and attacking volley (offensive) are easy because there is virtually no follow-through and a complete follow-through, respectively. The in-between - volleying or punching the ball softly back to an opponent's feet - is the most challenging volley to master. In this situation, there should be a short, confident follow-through. I say swing confidently because hesitating when following through is one of the most common errors players make. It can cause the ball to float too high or fall straight into the net. Decide what you are going to do and do it. Hesitation is deadly on any shot.

Let's get back to the follow-through. There should be some follow-through when volleying softly. How much follow-through is required depends on the speed and height of the ball the opponents hit. In general, the faster the ball comes towards you, the less follow-through is needed. When the ball is flying fast, the opponents are supplying the power. So keep the follow-through short and slow down the swing to avoid hitting high, returning quickly to the ready position.

Conversely, the slower the ball comes towards you, the more necessary follow-through becomes. Remember that following through more does not mean swinging harder. In practice, be mindful of how much follow-through you need to consistently hit down to your opponent's feet. Keep adjusting to dial in exactly how much to follow through is required in any situation.

Wrist Lock

Most players should make contact with a firm wrist when volleying. There are many volleying techniques and grips, but keep the wrist locked throughout the shot for higher consistency. There are exceptions depending on a player's style, but in general, utilizing too much wrist usually introduces inconsistency. Instead, try keeping every shot the same. The easiest way to do this is to keep the wrist locked. You might use more wrist when attacking at a higher level, but at first, improve consistency by reducing the number of moving components.

Where to Aim the Volley

Depending on the situation, sometimes there is time to aim, and sometimes there is not. In a fast volley exchange, the primary objective is to volley low to the opponent's feet and inhibit their ability to attack. Don't worry about aiming for the weaker player or hitting their more vulnerable side. That should happen only from a neutral or offensive position. In the wise words of a viral YouTube video, "ain't nobody got time for that."

When the pace slows and you have time to aim, consider a few strategic places on the court.

1. The Crosscourt Player

2. The player Further from the NVZ Line

3. The Weaker Player's Weaker Side

4. Open Spaces

5. The Hesitation Zone

6. The Player Closest to You

Let's go through each of these scenarios and explain why.

The Crosscourt Player

Hitting to the crosscourt player does a couple of things. First, the crosscourt player is further away, making it easier to place the ball at their feet while maintaining a margin for error. Second, the ball takes longer to travel crosscourt, buying time to prepare for the next shot. Note that the advice to volley crosscourt is primarily meant for a defensive or neutral position. In other words, volley crosscourt when contacting the ball below the net, as the person further away from you is a safer option. This gives you the best chance of hitting the ball to their feet, getting you out of trouble, or at least buy some time. When attacking, instead hit the person directly in front of you. This takes away precious time and the ability to react.

The Player Further from the NVZ Line

Sometimes, an opponent retreats from the NVZ line because they do not feel comfortable or do not know how to play strategically. Whatever the reason, this is an opportunity to press the advantage and keep pressure on the player further from the NVZ line. They will have a more challenging time keeping a dink or volley low, allowing you to continue attacking and eventually win the point. Moreover, because they are further away, it is easier to volley towards their feet, giving you some additional margin of error. Most opponents will eventually hit the net, out, or high by forcing them to continue hitting from low and behind the NVZ line.

The Weaker Player's Weaker Side

Often a particular side (most often the backhand) of one

specific player is clearly weaker. Observe details like this, especially in a tournament situation, and exploit those weaknesses. It can win you points at crucial junctures of a match. In recreational games, take the opposite approach and play to the stronger player's weaker side. If you are feeling particularly bold (or you are the best player on the court), you could even play to the stronger player's better side. Playing to the stronger player in recreational games allows you to improve faster. The important thing is that you continue to aim for a particular spot, improving accuracy. Remember, though, only aim for a specific target when playing from a neutral or offensive position. The primary goal is survival in a defensive situation, so keep the ball low without aiming for a particular place.

Open Spaces

Sometimes you have successfully moved the opponents around the court, forcing them to either become too close together, too far apart, or leave open spaces. Alternatively, there could be open spaces simply by how far apart the opponents stand from each other or when one arrives at the NVZ line first. Hitting into open spaces, especially down the middle, is effective for several reasons. First, you may hit a clean winner if the opponent cannot reach the ball. Even if one player retrieves the ball, hitting while moving is always more complicated than hitting from a stationary position. Whenever possible, make the opponents move at least one step in either direction to keep them uncomfortable and constantly moving. Aiming to an open space in the middle of the court can also cause confusion or miscommunication. Sometimes they have not talked about who should hit a ball in the middle, or one player hesitates. They react too late, or maybe neither player even attempts to hit the ball. Especially when the opponents have never played together, this is a potential weakness to identify and exploit.

The Hesitation Zone

I often tell players to aim for the "hesitation zone." This is the area where the opponent must decide whether to hit a dink or a volley, resulting in a brief moment of hesitation. Think of the hesitation zone in this way: When the ball is hit low or high, deciding whether to hit a dink or volley is easy because you simply hit the shot that comes to you. However, when the ball is directed somewhere between, the opponent must actively decide which shot to hit. Many players have a tendency to retreat, let the ball bounce, and dink. If the opponents do this, you have successfully pushed them back from the NVZ line. Often, players volley but hesitate or panic, hitting the ball too hard, too high, or straight into the net. When in an offensive or neutral position, try aiming for this hesitation zone. It is one of the best ways to make the opponents uncomfortable or uncertain about which shot to hit, forcing discomfort, therefore creating errors.

The Player Closest to You

We said to hit volleys crosscourt from a defensive or neutral position earlier. In contrast, hit volleys down the line towards the closer player when attacking. In an offensive position, you have already gained control of the point. Hitting aggressively at the closer player leaves them little reaction time and keeps up the pressure. Even if they return the ball, it is often too high, allowing you to continue attacking the closer player and taking even more time away.

When to Attack

Players often ask how high of a ball they should attack. In other words, at what point do you go ahead and attack the ball vs. playing it safe, setting up the shot, and waiting for a better attempt? Of course, the answer depends on the situation, your body, comfort level, and stronger side, which we will discuss subsequently.

First, a general rule of thumb. Contacting the ball below the knees is a red light. Do not attack. It is preferable to return the ball softly but strategically, set up the next shot, and wait for a better opportunity. Attacking from a red light position below the knees leads to greater risk, raising the likelihood of hitting the ball into the net, out, or into the opponent's strike zone. Contacting the ball between the knees and the waist is a yellow light; proceed with caution. Attack sometimes, but mostly be patient. It depends on the opponents' strength, speed of the ball, and side (whether hitting a forehand or backhand). Some opponents like playing fast, so attacking a neutral ball ends up playing into their strength. Others are not ready, so it's best to surprise them by attacking a yellow light ball. It also depends on the speed of the ball because hitting a slow ball aggressively is much easier than hitting a ball coming fast. Finally, it depends on the side because attacking a neutral ball with a forehand could be intelligent pickleball, while the backhand could be risky. Finally, a ball above the waist is a green light; attack. You have earned the right to play aggressively, so don't let the opponents back into the point. Prioritize placement over speed by hitting it to their feet, but keep the pressure on the opponents.

Staying at the NVZ Line

As mentioned previously, remaining near the NVZ line is essential for effective volleying. Retreating from the NVZ line makes it easier for opponents to hit to your feet and is not recommended except in a truly desperate situation. After retreating, the shot must now be executed further away, lowering the chances of successfully placing it back at the opponents' feet. In addition, you must cover more distance by moving back and forth to and from the NVZ line. This can lead to getting caught out of position, fatigue, and leaving more open spaces. Therefore, stay close to the NVZ line whenever possible. It may feel uncomfortable or scary at first, but it will bring you more success than playing from further back in the court.

Distance from your Partner

Another question often asked is, "how close should I stand to my partner when volleying?" Remember that when your opponents are hitting an offensive shot, the most straightforward place for them to aim is the middle of the court. To take away their easiest shot, position yourselves to always cover the middle. This means that when both players' paddles are outstretched, they should touch or be just out of reach. Removing the easiest shot from the opponents forces them to hit straight at you or attempt a more difficult shot near the sideline, increasing the odds of missing wide.

Anticipation

Earlier in this chapter, we discussed a study that cited that elite athletes don't actually have faster reaction times than ordinary people. Preparation partly gives them seemingly quicker reflexes, but the other component is anticipation. Since there is still far too little academic research on pickleball, we will use tennis as our example. To quote The Sports Gene again,

Elite athletes need less time and visual information to know what will happen in the future, and, without knowing it, zero in on critical visual information... Top tennis players could discern from the minuscule pre-serve shifts of an opponent's torso whether a shot was going to their forehand or backhand. In contrast, average players had to wait to see the motion of the racket, costing valuable response time.

How do you gain this mastery of anticipation? You guessed it, 10,000 hours. Even if you never become an elite athlete, it's still important to be aware of anticipating better. Attempt to remember the movements of a particular opponent and discern patterns in their play. For example, when they wind up with their forehand, do they always hit crosscourt? How are their feet positioned? How does their torso move? Try reading these subtle signs and moving a little earlier in that direction ahead of time. This gives you a better chance of returning the ball effectively. Another good example is to prepare to duck whenever the opponent takes a full backswing from the NVZ line, especially when they are in a defensive or neutral position. It will probably hit the back fence, so get out of the way.

Misdirection

Everyone anticipates so well at the highest levels of pickleball that it helps to employ some disguise tactics. This is where misdirection comes into play. Misdirection makes it look like you will hit in one direction, then change at the last second. Your body positioning, paddle angle, wind up, etc., all come into play when attempting to mislead the opponent. The most common and easiest misdirection is done by the paddle angle. To do this, try facing the paddle towards the person directly in front of you. They will think you are hitting to them. Then, at the last second, change the paddle direction by switching to the crosscourt player. Do this too often, and you have ruined any element of surprise, but it can be an effective tool for occasional deceit. The key is practice and knowing beforehand what you are going to do. Remember, hesitation kills. Hitting a no-disguise shot well is preferable to missing while attempting something fancy. Although misdirection in volleying is utilized frequently, it is probably easier when dinking, so we will discuss misdirection in more detail in the chapter on dinking.

Spin

Spin can also be a helpful tool when volleying. When hitting a ball anywhere above your knees, topspin effectively places the ball lower as it reaches the opponent. Balls hit with topspin also bounce differently than balls hit flat, so this can be an effective changeup when it bounces in front of the opponent. If one opponent is back, hitting towards them with topspin can push them even further back or cause them to make an error if the ball bounces differently than they expect. Utilizing slice provides more stability and control when volleying from a low position (below the knees). Additionally, when a ball hit with slice bounces, it stays lower and sometimes even skids, making it a difficult shot to return. Try experimenting with topspin and slice to see if either feels comfortable and in which situations you can best utilize them.

Lean In

One of the hardest things to do is lean into a speeding object flying towards your head. It goes against the natural instincts of self-preservation and survival. However, constantly flinching, jumping, or retreating is not an effective way to play pickleball. First, by not staying firmly on the ground, you lose stability. Stability in the legs is crucial when volleying and flinching, jumping, or backing up reduces both control and power as a result. Second, when leaning back, your paddle angle naturally tilts up. Instead of firing the ball back at the opponents' feet, it now floats upward, keeping you in defensive mode.

Although you cannot step in when volleying due to the NVZ line, lean forward. In addition to the increased stability and better paddle angle, leaning in communicates confidence; You are not afraid of the ball and will not back away. Instead of flinching when the opponents attack, prepare by leaning forward with your paddle in front. Hit a reset shot if the ball is low or counterattack if the ball is high. Even if you fail, you have communicated that you are not afraid. Imagine playing against one of the top pros. You would think twice about attacking them because you know they won't back down. Similarly, make the opponents think twice about attacking you because they know you will not retreat, and the ball will likely come right back at them.

Poaching

In the return of serve section, we discussed returning down the line to make it easier for your partner to get involved. Getting involved, AKA "poaching," means moving over to your partner's side to hit a volley. When your forehand is in the middle and your partner returns down the line, step toward the center. By doing this, it puts additional pressure on the opponents. They know that you are ready to poach if their drop shot goes high. As a result, they will try to avoid you, sometimes making mistakes. Another strategy is to wait until the opponents hit to move towards the center. This way, they do not know the poach is coming. Either way, put pressure on the opponents by making your presence known. Remember, pickleball is a mental game so make them think you might poach, even if you don't do it every time.

Poaching when your partner has not yet reached the NVZ line is effective for several reasons. First, because your partner is still in the back of the court or transition zone, you don't have to worry about who is going to hit the ball or about knocking them over. Second, many drop shots float high. If you let your partner take the next shot and it bounces before they can reach it, you have wasted an opportunity to take advantage of a high drop shot by letting the ball bounce. Whenever possible, take advantage by poaching and forcing the opponents to stay back. Communication is vital when poaching, though, so make sure your partner knows that you might poach given the right opportunity. If you poach into their half of the court, your partner needs to move over to cover the area you left empty.

Conclusion

To summarize the volley section, the most important concepts are keeping everything in front, not gripping the paddle too tight, and keeping the swing compact. Most players simply swing too big or too hard, leading to a loss of control. Even if you have to hit softly, make sure your volleys are landing at your opponent's feet so that they cannot attack you. If they cannot control the ball either, hitting their feet ensures that you will eventually receive a nice high ball to attack.

Chapter 7

The Dink

By Daniel

What comes to mind when you think of dinking? Perhaps kicking yourself for not being more patient? Hitting a floater that is promptly smashed back? Not exactly knowing what to do with the ball or where to hit? Or do you have a more positive image of winning points by outlasting your opponents and setting up the point to finish with a crisp winner? Confidence is often the only difference between these perspectives. From personal experience, when I play with doubt, my dinking game seems to vanish into thin air. Even though I was aggressive and putting pressure on my opponents just a few points before, with the flip of a switch, that confidence can desert me. Even at the elite level, dinking with confidence is a constant battle with your opponents and yourself. It takes practice, discipline, and a positive mentality. Not only must you practice, but you must also practice the right way. It is worth it, though, because you will become dangerous when theory and execution come together. Let's discuss some components of this shot that will take your dinking to the next level.

What is Dinking?

Before discussing the shot, let's first look at what precisely a dink is. Here is USA Pickleball's definition of a dink.

1. A soft shot hit on a bounce from the NVZ intended to arc over the net and land within the opposing NVZ either straight across or diagonally crosscourt.

2. An effective dink arcs downward as it crosses the net, creating a more difficult shot to return than a power shot.

3. Dinks that land close to the net are the most difficult to return because of the steep angle required to get the ball over the net.

4. Crosscourt dinks are easier because the net is lower in the center, and you can force their opponent off the court, potentially opening a hole.

5. Contact the ball in front of the body with the paddle face open, using a gentle lifting (pushing) motion.

6. The shot is soft and controlled with movement from the shoulder, no wrist break, and minimal or no backswing to avoid overpowering the ball.

7. Be patient. Continue to dink until the opponent makes a mistake. If the ball is hit too high, there is a good chance for a put-away shot.

That's a lot, but we will keep coming back to these, as they contain both important advice and common misconceptions about the dink. So let's clarify some misconceptions and hopefully start thinking about dinking differently. For now, my definition is the following:

A setup shot hit off the bounce from the NVZ line that is not an attempted winner.

That's it. Notice that dinking is primarily about the intention behind the shot. You are not trying to win the point outright. Instead, you should set up the point, waiting for either a ball to put away or for the opponents to miss. This waiting can take a long time, so you need the physical ability and proper mindset to keep the ball in play longer than the opponents. There are ways to put pressure on them, of course, and we will discuss those, but fundamentally, dinking is about outlasting your opponents. There is a lot to unpack here, so let's jump right in.

Ready Position

Let's begin with the ready position. I mentioned in the volley section that when standing at the NVZ line, you do not know whether the next ball coming will be a dink or a volley, forehand or backhand. Assuming one or the other by not preparing for all of these shots is a dangerous proposition. The fact that you just hit three dinks in a row means nothing. Note again that there is a difference here between assumption and anticipation. Assumption is guessing without preparation. Anticipation is an educated guess based on past experience combined with preparing for anything. Try to anticipate the opponent's next move but don't assume anything by failing to prepare.

As I said, you don't know whether the next shot will be a dink or a volley. Therefore, your ready position should be the same for both shots. Slightly or heavily favor the backhand side depending on the situation and always keep the paddle in front. For a more thorough explanation or refresher, refer to the volley section. For now, suffice to say that you must prepare for both possibilities, dinking or volleying.

One common tendency that leads to unpreparedness is not returning the paddle to the ready position after hitting a dink. Because dinking occurs after the ball bounces, the contact point for dinks is typically lower than for volleys. You must adjust to where the ball is, so this is not a problem as long as you bend your knees and lift the ball. However, many players keep the paddle there after bringing the paddle down to a low contact point and finishing the shot. This occurs from the mistaken assumption that the next ball will come to the same place, laziness, habit, or without the offending player even noticing. If the next shot does happen to be a dink, you get away with it. You got lucky, but unfortunately, this actually reinforces a bad habit. Sooner or later, you will be caught off guard with a fast volley. When that happens, the paddle is not in the ready position, getting you into trouble because you were not prepared. Typically your paddle head is down, or you do not make contact in front of your body, neither of which is ideal. This is often when the infamous "chicken wing" occurs. Sometimes you return the ball successfully, but you often miss or set up the opponents for a winner. It could have been prevented by simply returning the paddle to the ready position in front.

Short Backswing

Maintaining a short backswing is useful when dinking for a couple of reasons. First, this is a controlled shot from short range; what is needed is more control, not more power. You don't need much backswing even on a drop shot from further back, so it's really unnecessary when dinking. Shortening the swing will help keep the ball low and drop down to the opponent's feet. Another tendency when dinking, especially when pulled out wide, is to take the paddle further back. Perhaps you think you need more power, or it feels like you are buying yourself more time by hitting the ball from a contact point behind your body. In reality, what happens is that the ball gets behind you and drops lower, pulling you off the NVZ line and creating a more challenging shot. Remember, something that buys you more time also buys the opponents more time. Instead, when you must move to hit a dink, try cutting it off early by taking the ball in front of you with little to no backswing. You might have to hit the ball off the short hop, but you will have less distance to cover, and it will take time away from the opponents. It will also be much easier to return to your original position on the court to prepare for the next shot because you have not stepped back from the line.

Follow Through

Much like other shots, the follow-through is more important than the backswing. Always finish the shot by swinging through past the contact point. Of course, the follow-through should be shorter and slower when dinking than when hitting the drop shot. However, create the habit of intentionally following through and finishing every shot. Many mistakes are made just by stopping the paddle. Following through increases the contact time between the paddle and ball. This increases control, as the ball stays on the paddle longer rather than quickly popping off. You don't need to follow through all the way to where your shoulder touches your chin, but make sure the paddle continues to move forward after the ball leaves. It might feel uncomfortable at first like the ball will sail high, but in reality, swinging through actually helps keep the ball lower because you gain more control.

Swing Softer and Slower

Swinging hard when dinking leads to disaster. Most players simply swing with too much force and speed, hitting their dinks flat and hard instead of soft and arching. Hitting hard and flat is fine if the dink is hit perfectly, but the problem is that many of these balls will clip the net or sail high. You simply do not need that much power for the ball to land at the opponent's feet. Again, imagine it's an egg you don't want to crack. Be as gentle as possible. When you have an attackable ball, go ahead and smash the egg. There is not much middle ground in pickleball. Go soft or hard but not in between. My dad likes to say, "go hard, go soft or go home."

Wrist Lock

Keep your wrist firm to avoid floppiness and inconsistency. Although some players coming from sports that use a lot of wrist can employ it effectively, most pickleball players should maintain a locked wrist. This is true for dinking more than perhaps any other shot. Locking the wrist allows you to utilize the larger muscles, primarily the shoulder. This produces a more consistent and repeatable motion, making you a more effective dinkers. Especially in defensive mode, dinking is about repeating the same uniform swinging motion every time to get back to the point. Don't try anything fancy from defensive mode. Keeping the swing consistent by locking the wrist is the best way to achieve that objective. I know it is tempting to hit a beautiful topspin forehand winner or put tons of slice on the backhand, but neither of these are high percentage shots, especially from a defensive position. Just hit the ball back and do the fancy stuff when you have more time.

Bend the Knees

Because of the low contact point necessarily associated with dinking, you must bring the paddle down one way or another. This can be accomplished by bending at the waist or bending at the knees. Bending at the knees makes it easier to lift the ball from underneath, swinging in a low to high motion. In addition, it is a more balanced, stable, and athletic position that allows for adjustments and better footwork. Once you have bent at the waist, you are planted in cement with no ability to move your feet. Your head is pointed down, meaning you can no longer use peripheral vision. You now must use your wrist to open the paddle angle. And if the next shot floats high, you must straighten out before hitting the next shot. Bending at the waist occurs more often when a player is lazy or tired and should be avoided as much as possible. Bending at the knees feels like more work (because it is), but it is also the more balanced, consistent, and effective shot that will win you more points long term.

Paddle Angle

This is similar to the paddle angle discussion in the volley section. The lower the contact point, the more upward facing or open-faced the paddle must be. The higher the ball, the more downward-facing or close-faced the paddle must be. Making slight adjustments to the paddle angle depending on the height of the ball is a crucial skill for developing your pickleball game. When you hit a ball too low or too high, observe the paddle angle to see what went wrong and make an adjustment the next time.

Footwork

There is a great deal of disagreement on what constitutes proper footwork when dinking, with even pros exhibiting vastly different styles and amounts of footwork. Of course, this is not gospel truth, but I will give you some general guidelines to consider when dinking.

Remember that even if you don't end up moving, you always should retain the ability to move if needed. This means staying on the balls of your feet in an athletic stance (knees slightly bent, shoulder-width apart) so that you can move if necessary to stay balanced when you hit the next shot. You do not want cement feet or being entirely planted with the feet too close together or too far apart. When that happens, you start lunging for balls, getting off-balance, hitting behind your body, and not returning to the line for the next shot, none of which help win the point.

The most common debate regarding movement when dinking is whether to cross the feet (picture tennis) or maintain an open stance. Crossing the feet over is called a closed stance, while not crossing (like when hitting a volley) is called an open stance. I would say that your personal preference is essential to keep in mind. What feels more comfortable to you? Many players find it easier to keep the same form between volleys and dinks and therefore prefer an open stance, while others like the closed stance from a tennis background. Another consideration is, do you have time to cross over? When I am in a defensive position, I try not to cross my feet because I don't have enough time. Even if I sometimes have time, it's more challenging to return to my original position on the court after crossing my feet. When I am in a neutral or offensive position and can take my time,

I often cross my feet, get low, and try hitting a more aggressive, low dink that skids after bouncing on their side. If the ball is hit far enough away from you, you may have no choice but to cross your feet and stretch to reach the ball. If that happens, attempt to dink cross court and soft, buying yourself enough time to get back into the point. Your partner probably needs to hurry over and help cover your side of the court, so make sure to communicate, as you don't want to leave open spaces, especially down the middle.

Where to Hit the Dink

Before discussing the location, remember that the purpose of dinking is to set up the point rather than hitting an outright winner. Before overthinking the spot to aim, remember that the primary objective is to keep the ball in play and unattackable. In other words, don't screw up! I don't have any data to back this up, but I guess that more than 80% of pickleball players cannot consistently hit 10 dinks in a row. This means that by keeping the ball low and in, no matter where you aim, you can beat 80% of pickleball players at the dinking game. Hopefully, that is an encouraging thought. If not, I hope it inspires you to practice.

Adjusting to the Situation

Once you can consistently hit more than 10 dinks in a row, start thinking about the location of those dinks. Like the volley section, start thinking about the situation: defensive, neutral, or offensive, and adjust accordingly.

To remind you, defensive mode is when you are being pushed back, forced to move, in trouble, or pressured/ uncomfortable. Neutral mode is when neither team has a clear advantage, and offensive mode is when your opponents are pushed back, forced to move, in trouble, or pressured/uncomfortable.

In defensive mode, AKA survival mode, all you should try to do is survive. Like USA Pickleball's advice, try to return the ball into your opponents' NVZ so they cannot keep attacking. Making the ball bounce on the opponents' side will buy you more time than allowing them to volley. When in defensive mode, the immediate objective is to return to neutral mode, where neither team has an advantage. Only then can you start making things happen. When you are in trouble or on the defensive, think of driving a manual car. Before you can shift gears, you must always go through neutral.

The temptation is attempting too much from defensive mode. Going for a winner, trying to redirect the dink down the line, aiming for your opponent's weaker side, or playing too aggressively from a defensive position all increase risk. I cannot tell you how many times I have seen players forced wide on their backhand side, hitting hard and attempting a perfect down-the-line winner. It's spectacular when executed perfectly, but how often does it actually succeed? Maybe 10% of the time. Those are not odds you would take to Vegas, so don't expect it to work in pickleball. Instead, simplify defensive mode by telling yourself just to make the ball bounce cross court in the opponents' NVZ and stay alive. Wait to make something happen after you transition from defensive to neutral. Survive for one more shot and live to die another day. Try to give your opponent at least one more opportunity to miss: Often, they will do just that.

In defensive mode especially, hitting crosscourt is typically the wisest option. First, as USA Pickleball mentions, the net is lower in the middle, meaning fewer net errors. The most important reason is that you gain a better margin for error by hitting crosscourt. What does this mean? When dinking down the line (straight across from you), there is a distance of only 14 feet to the opponent. There is even less distance if they stand at the NVZ line, are tall, and lean forward. Even a slightly high ball is returned aggressively and quickly, giving you little time to react and often catching you out of position. To prevent this, you must hit lower, increasing the likelihood of missing in the net. However, when dinking crosscourt, there is typically a distance of 16-20 feet to the opponent. You can now aim higher over the net and still retain the ability to bring the ball down to the opponent's feet. In addition, if you happen to hit the ball too high, you have more time to recover, increasing your chances of getting back in the point. Dinking crosscourt is a great general guideline for all your dinks, but it is especially helpful in defensive mode to get out of trouble.

Let's move to neutral and offensive modes, which we will lump together in this section. Remember that the opponents either have no advantage in these situations or are scrambling to get back in the point. This gives you more time to pick a spot, be aggressive, push them back, forcing them to move, or make them feel pressured/uncomfortable. The best strategy for dinking in neutral/offensive modes is to keep switching it up so that you are not predictable and the opponents never become comfortable. The importance of keeping them guessing and off-balance is the main reason I disagree with conventional wisdom in USA Pickleball's dink definition, "to aim for within the opponents' NVZ and to make the ball bounce as close to the net as possible." This advice is reasonable in defensive mode but predictable and unproductive in neutral or offensive modes because it fails to continue pressuring the opponents. In fact, it helps them get out of trouble.

Instead, I like to think of my shot placement as an XY axis. You can make opponents uncomfortable by moving them side to side, but you can also make them uncomfortable by moving them forwards and backward. After hitting a short dink closer to the net, try hitting a deeper shot towards their feet to force them back. A dink does not have to land in the NVZ to be effective. Not all opponents will retreat when faced with a deeper dink. If they do, though, it can benefit you because they have moved away from the NVZ line, opening up space on the court. Even if they can return to the NVZ line, they may be tired or out of balance when hitting the next shot. If they choose instead to volley when faced with a deep dink, that's fine too. Many players cannot effectively control volleys, floating the ball high or hitting the net. Knowing they cannot control the ball, some will hit aggressively from a low contact point, making more mistakes or floating the ball into your attackable zone. Varying between short and deep dinks makes them go back and forth between dinking and volleying. This inhibits their ability to relax and become comfortable. Remember to continue mixing it up in neutral or offensive mode, never letting the opponents off the hook.

If depth is the X-axis, the Y-axis is how you move the opponents from side to side. In offensive or neutral mode, hitting crosscourt is also practical because of the better margin for error. Because you can aim higher above the net while still hitting the ball at your opponent's feet, you can be more aggressive when hitting crosscourt without taking any additional risk. Hitting crosscourt does not mean aiming for the same spot every time, though. Conventional wisdom (once again included in USA Pickleball's definition) states that the reason to hit crosscourt is to force your opponent off the court by hitting wide, opening up the center. The problem with this philosophy is that you must keep hitting wider to move your opponent, aiming closer to the sideline. Sometimes you will hit the ball too wide, setting up an ATP (around the post) or hitting out, wasting all the effort of setting up the point.

A better strategy is to alternate between hitting wide and hitting towards the center. First, it is always harder to hit a ball while moving, and second, alternating placement makes it easier to open spaces on the court. Alternating your dink placement ensures the opponent will constantly be moving and uncomfortable. Margin for error applies to the sideline as much as the net. Aiming too close to the sideline decreases your margin, so play it safe by not aiming for the lines. Remember, in many cases, just hitting 10 dinks in a row - wherever those dinks land - is enough to win the point.

Additionally, alternating dink placement means becoming unpredictable. Don't be afraid to experiment between wide and center, shallow and deep, to keep your opponents guessing. Prioritize consistency, but keep changing what you do and be unpredictable whenever safely possible. Eventually, you will be rewarded with opportunities to attack, or better yet, some free points when the opponents miss.

Spin

Both topspin and slice can be practical tools for mixing it up or putting pressure on the opponents. Like my advice in previous sections, I suggest gaining the ability to hit consistently without additional spin before attempting more complex shots. Generally, hitting with slice is more natural on the backhand side, although some players do superbly from the forehand side. Bend your knees, create a paddle face conducive to hitting slice, and swing forward through the ball instead of chopping down. Going for too much slice by chopping down leads to the ball going straight into the net. Instead, swing in a flat or slightly upward motion, lifting, so the ball goes over the net.

Topspin is more complicated than slice for most players. When dinking, it is primarily utilized on the forehand side and only when the ball bounces high. Roll through the ball without using too much wrist. In most cases, you will still need to swing from low to high to ensure the ball goes over the net. Trying to use topspin too often, from a defensive position, from an insufficiently high contact point, or trying to put too much spin on the ball are all common mistakes. Don't attempt a too tricky shot, as difficult shots lead to more errors. As always, master the simple shot before moving onto the riskier, more challenging alternative and only attempt more complex shots from neutral or offensive mode.

Misdirection

The higher the level in pickleball, the better the opponents will anticipate the next move and know where you are hitting. Disguising shots is a valuable tool to keep opponents guessing and uncomfortable. Within misdirection, there are two types: paddle angle misdirection and body misdirection. High-level pickleball players employ one or both, so they can be an essential weapon in developing your own pickleball game.

In the volley section, we briefly discussed paddle angle misdirection and mentioned it is the easiest and more common type. Paddle angle misdirection means you "show" the opponents one paddle angle, then change it at the last second. For example, show the opponents a crosscourt dink, then switch to down the line just before contact. Even if they retrieve the ball, opponents may be caught unprepared, occasionally winning a free point. At the very least, they know you might do it again, keeping them honest by forcing them to cover all parts of the court. This is an excellent strategy when playing mixed doubles, and the male player positions himself in the middle of the court. Disguising your shot then hitting behind the male player prevents him from poaching and opens up the court. You should only dink down the line from a neutral or offensive position, so a bit of misdirection increases the likelihood that you can catch the opponents off guard or keep them guessing and uncomfortable.

I want to emphasize the importance of knowing where you are hitting before contact when implementing misdirection. Misdirection is not the same as hesitation. Even though you switch at the last second, you must know where the shot is going before hitting. Know where you will hit the ball and only misdirect with intentionality when in neutral or offensive modes. Attempting to misdirect in defensive mode is too risky and low percentage, inviting more mistakes. Too often, players use misdirection in conjunction with hesitation, meaning they decide to misdirect at the last second because they cannot decide. This leads to errors as well. If you cannot choose where to hit the ball, just go back crosscourt.

Body misdirection means turning your body in a way that makes your opponents believe you will be hitting one way, then switching at the last moment. This is the more difficult type, so I recommend only trying it after mastering the paddle angle misdirection. However, because fewer players employ it, it can come as a surprise. It is easier to utilize body misdirection when dinking if you turn your shoulders. Typically, the shoulders turn more when hitting down the line than crosscourt. By turning the shoulders more, your opponents will believe that you are hitting down the line. Then, at the last second, turn your body so that you hit crosscourt, hopefully catching the opponents unaware.

The Short Hop

Some higher-level players employ the short hop rather than waiting for the ball to bounce up to its highest point. This means dinking right after the ball bounces so that you don't have to volley or back up, with the additional advantage of taking time away from the opponents. Of course, you need to bend your knees and get low to hit this shot effectively. Be aware that the short hop brings the disadvantage of having a low contact point, though. It requires more control to hit from a low position, bring the ball over the net and back down to the opponent's feet, which is why we include it in the high-level dinking section. Being able to hit a short hop or a regular dink can keep the opponents guessing and uncomfortable, however, so it is advantageous if you can learn to use it.

Conclusion

Mastering the dink is essential to becoming an advanced pickleball player. Remember, the primary objective of dinking is to set up the point, so don't try to do too much. Simply outlasting your opponent is the best way to win a point. Remember that you need less power and backswing than you think, so keep the swing compact, slow, and even. Finally, this requires practice like every other shot, so get out there and work on your dinking!

Chapter 8

The Reset

By Daniel

The reset shot is a difficult concept because it is not a particular shot (dink or volley), and it is not hit from a single location on the court. Instead, it is a shot that is utilized whenever the opponents attack. In other words, resetting is what you do in defensive mode when the opponents are smashing or attacking. The idea is to take an aggressive ball and hit it back softly at their feet so they cannot continue attacking. This is the best (often only) way to get out of trouble. It is one of the most challenging shots to master, though, because the team resetting is already in serious trouble. Otherwise, they wouldn't need to reset in the first place. It is difficult to control the ball that is hit aggressively at your feet. Too often, a player who should be resetting swings hard, getting themselves into even more trouble. Understand that you will not successfully reset every time; not even the pros can do that. However, being aware of the shot, staying calm, and attempting it more often when in trouble will raise the number of successful resets and therefore points won. Even an imperfect reset is better than an outright error because it forces the opponents to at least hit one more shot, allowing them to make a mistake.

Ultimately resetting is a mentality. You seldom should retreat unless you can do it before the opponent strikes the ball, and definitely never give up on a point. As long as the rally continues, there is still a chance. This mentality will help you retrieve more balls and win more points. Resetting is also one of the most exciting ways to win a point, coming back from the brink and turning the point around in your favor. Of course, everyone gets into trouble, but high-level players can more consistently snatch victory from the jaws of defeat. Let's discuss the reset here so you will really understand it.

Primary Reset Scenarios

There are two primary situations in which the reset shot is used:

After a high drop shot

After hitting a drop shot high, the serving team should not move forward (unless they have a death wish). The impending attack is coming when the drop shot floats too high, so prepare as quickly as possible. Preparation includes:

1. Stopping completely and doing a quick hop called a quick step.

2. Getting into an athletic position (knees bent, on the toes).

3. Favoring the backhand side (remember this from the volley section).

By stopping and preparing, you give yourself the best chance to successfully reset and move forward toward the NVZ line on the next shot or even a couple of shots later. The nice thing about the reset shot from this position in the court is that you have some time to react before the ball arrives. Because the opponents are further away, the chances of at least making contact are high with the correct preparation. After all, you only have to cover your half of the court. So there still is a good chance of getting back into the point. The key is to prepare early, stay low, and don't panic. If you have time to panic, you have time to prepare. One of the hardest things in pickleball is to relax when the opponents are smashing a ball down your throat but relaxing is one of the most important aspects of a successful reset. Make sure to cover the middle so that the opponents have to aim toward the sideline to hit a clean winner, taking a greater risk.

After an unsuccessful dink or volley

Often in a dink or volley exchange, you or your partner (it's always your partner's fault, right?) hit the ball too high, allowing the opponents to attack. This situation is much direr, as impending doom is hammering down much closer to you. You only have time to hold the paddle on the backhand side and attempt to block the ball back. Again, prepare early by bending the knees, leaning forward, and keeping the paddle in a backhand position. Try to anticipate the opponent's attack based on the height of the ball. Generally, the higher the contact point on the opponents' side, the lower the contact point will be on your side. Here is the bad news: you will not successfully retrieve most of these shots. After all, the odds are stacked heavily in favor of the attacking team. Here is the good news: retrieving even one more ball than before is progress and can translate to winning more points in a game. This could be important in a critical juncture like the end of an important match and sometimes make the difference between winning and losing. Of course, it is always preferable to stay out of trouble in the first place, but know that it is possible to get out of trouble sometimes with the right mentality.

Placement

Don't worry about which opponent to hit towards. There is no time to think strategically other than simply keeping the ball low. The goal is to block the ball back to the opponent's feet, into their unattackable zone, and allow your team to get back into the point. Ensure the paddle is pointed slightly upward and absorb the shock without supplying more energy to the ball. In other words, just let the ball hit your paddle. The ball will bounce over the net toward the opponent's feet with the correct paddle angle. Don't swing because the opponents are supplying all the power needed. After resetting successfully, think about placement only from a neutral or offensive position.

Lean in

It seems counterintuitive to lean or step into a flying object speeding towards you. However, forward momentum is crucial to executing a successful reset shot. As discussed in other sections, stepping back opens the paddle angle, removes control, and takes you further away from the objective of playing from the NVZ line. In addition, flinching or running away never helps you hit a clean, consistent shot. Instead of stepping back while hitting, if necessary, take a step back before the ball arrives, time permitting. Once the opponent strikes the ball, lean in or step forward while making contact with the ball. It is preferable not to retreat, but if unavoidable, retreat only before the ball is struck by your opponent, then move forward as you hit the ball. Strategically retreating applies only to reset shots from the NVZ line, though. For a reset shot from further back in the court, there is plenty of time/space and no need to retreat. Simply prepare where you are standing, then step or lean forward and step into the next ball.

Wrist Lock

Similar to previous sections, a loose wrist is often the cause of inconsistency. Lock the wrist to create a stable paddle surface, as a floppy wrist and therefore paddle lead to mistakes. This also makes it much easier to strike the ball in the middle of the paddle, leading to better control.

Some players attempt to slice or topspin when resetting: for most, this is trying too much. Simplify the shot as much as possible by striking the ball with a flat surface. Keep your stroke as compact and close to your body as possible to strike the ball cleanly and reduce errors.

Paddle in Front

There should be little to no backswing when resetting. For one, there is insufficient time to take a large backswing, particularly when resetting from the NVZ line. Additionally, the opponent is hitting hard, so typically, there is no need to supply more power. Instead, position the paddle in front of the body and block the ball back with little to no swing. The only time you might need some forward swing is from mid-court, especially if the opponent doesn't hit particularly hard. Even then, you can swing forward, but you do not need a large backswing. Beat the ball to where it is going by placing the paddle there first and letting the ball hit your paddle. Bend your knees and get low before the ball arrives so you are prepared early. Knowing where the ball is coming requires some anticipation, so try noticing the opponents' tendencies and make an educated guess where they will attack. Cover the middle first to take away the easiest shot. Remember that you are trying to control the ball and slow it down, so there is no need to take a giant swing.

Less Follow Through

We mentioned the need to follow through fully and finish

the swing in other sections. This is true when having to actively generate power. However, the opponent usually hits hard when you are resetting, supplying all the power and energy needed. Therefore, a full followthrough is not necessary, as most of the time, you are actually attempting to decelerate the speed of the ball. You could use a short, abbreviated followthrough when resetting from further back, but that is the most you would ever need. In most cases, simply allowing the paddle to absorb the energy without any followthrough is enough to clear the net. Anything more could cause the ball to sail high into the opponent's strike zone.

Paddle Angle

The lower the contact point, the more open or upward facing the paddle angle. The higher the contact point, the more closed or downward-facing the paddle angle. This is true of any shot but particularly important when hitting a reset shot, where even a slight change in paddle angle could have drastic consequences. After hitting a reset shot too high or low, learn from it and try adjusting the paddle angle slightly the next time. Hitting a little too high is preferable to catching the net, but fine-tune the reset shot by learning from each mistake. The combination of swing speed and paddle angle dictates the height of the ball, so constantly tweak the formula until you get it right.

Here is a tip on paddle angle and preparing early: the higher the opponent's contact point when attacking, the lower you will typically have to get down to hit the ball.

If your opponent is hitting an overhead smash from a high contact point, prepare early by bending your knees and opening the paddle face as soon as you see the ball go high. They will most likely hit down to your feet so prepare before the ball arrives by bending the knees and opening the paddle angle. Contrarily, when you are at the NVZ line, and the opponents are attacking from a contact point around their waist or chest, it is not as crucial to bend all the way down. It is almost impossible for them to hit down to your feet so just bend the knees slightly. Finally, if they are hitting hard from around their feet, learn to duck. If the ball is hit hard and still rising when it gets to you, chances are the ball is going out. Learning patterns like this will improve anticipation and make it feel like you have faster reflexes.

Soft Hands

No, we are not recommending you use Dove moisturizer, although that's totally up to you. Soft hands mean gaining a better feel for the paddle and how the ball flies off it. It starts with grip strength employed when hitting a reset shot. Out of fear, habit, or even unconsciously, most players grip the paddle too hard, especially when the ball is coming hard at them. This is understandable since a ball is being smashed at them, but it leads to the ball flying off the paddle with a great deal of pop, flying off so that you can control it. Pop is excellent when attacking, but you are trying to slow down the ball when resetting. Grip the paddle loosely, as this gives you greater control and feel, leading to better reset shots. If grip strength were on a scale of 1-10, grip the paddle somewhere between a 3-5 when resetting. Hold tight enough so that the paddle does not wobble or move in your hand when the ball strikes it, but not so tight that the ball flies off the paddle before you have a chance to control it.

Reset Mentality

I cannot emphasize enough the importance of playing with confidence instead of fear. Fear leads to leaning back, stepping away, flinching, jumping, a lack of preparation, and/or slower reflexes. Use that time instead to prepare and give yourself the best chance of retrieving the ball. No one likes getting hit, but early preparation - not freezing up or retreating is the best way to avoid it. Instead, bend the knees, place the paddle in front and lean in. This gives you the best chance of successfully resetting and having a chance at winning the point.

Of the previously mentioned negative tendencies, flinching is particularly common. It is only natural to shy away from an object flying at you. However, if you can overcome that natural instinct and lean forward, you will drastically increase the chances of a successful reset. In practice, have a partner or a ball machine fire balls at you from close, medium, and long ranges. When you know a ball is coming fast, it is easier to lean forward and practice good habits. This will make doing the same in a game or tournament situation easier.

Move Forward After the Shot

When hitting a reset shot from anywhere behind the NVZ

line, always be prepared to move forward after hitting. Too many players hit a successful reset then admire their shot, wasting the opportunity to move forward. Always expect to move forward. Even after hitting a mediocre or lousy reset, move a couple of steps forward to get closer to the goal of playing from the NVZ line. Another benefit is that the opponents see you moving and know that they have to hit a good shot for it to go to your feet. Even if they hit it successfully, you want to get into their head as much as possible by putting pressure on them. Pickleball is such a mental game that sometimes, these slight movements can make a difference.

For a visual explanation of some of these concepts, check out the High-Performance Pickleball courses' reset section or YouTube video on the reset shot:

https://www.youtube.com/watch?v=16cN1uVdl2s&t=11s

Also, watch my dad's video on taking pace off the ball.

http://www.pickleballchannel.com/PB411-Pace-Off-Ball-Scott-Moore

Conclusion

The reset shot is, without a doubt, the most challenging shot in pickleball. In addition, it comes up in every game, so it's a shot you are definitely going to see more of. The mentality of not being afraid, combined with the preparation, will help you master this shot. Make sure to go out and drill the correct way to be ready and not scared in a game situation. Remember, never give up because the point is never over until the fat lady sings (or perhaps, in this case, until the fat ref calls the score).

Chapter 9

The Lob & Overhead

By Daniel

The Lob

The lob is often viewed as a last-ditch effort, a hail mary shot hit more from hope and wishful thinking than any realistic expectation of success. As a result, many players hit the shot from a defensive position, believing they have no alternative. Granted, it is true that hitting a lob in a desperate circumstance does buy you time. But it is not a fair exchange when buying time comes at the expense of a subsequent smash. This section will discuss the merits of the offensive lob, along with some techniques and strategies to help you think about the shot in a new light.

What Is It?

The lob is a high shot that attempts to hit over the

opponent's outstretched paddle. Ideally, they cannot reach the ball, which goes over their head and bounces within a few feet of the baseline. Hitting over the opponents' outstretched paddle means the ideal height for a lob depends on the opponents' height and reach. Hitting too low leads to being smashed while hitting too high provides them ample time to run back and retrieve the shot. An ideal lob goes a foot or two above the opponent's outstretched paddle, so they can't jump or easily back up and hit it. Done correctly, a lob becomes difficult to attack, let alone retrieve.

The Offensive Lob

USA Pickleball describes both defensive and offensive lobs in their shot definition. We are going to advocate forgetting about the defensive lob in most situations. Hit a drop shot instead if you have time to lob from a defensive position. They take the exact same amount of time. Why only lob from an offensive or neutral position? Remember that defensive mode is when you are being pushed back, forced to move, in trouble, pressured/uncomfortable, or out of position away from the NVZ line. Neutral mode is when neither team has a clear advantage, and offensive mode is when your opponents are pushed back, forced to move, in trouble, or pressured/uncomfortable.

There are two primary reasons to only lob offensively. First, hopefully, we agree that pickleball should be played from the NVZ line whenever possible. When one team positions itself at the NVZ line and the other team stands further back, the team at the NVZ line gains a significant advantage. The further away from the NVZ line, the less chance the team will win the point. Lobbing offensively when all players are already at the NVZ line forces the opponents to play from behind the NVZ line, raising the probability your team will win the point. If you had a 50/50 chance of winning the point with everyone playing from the NVZ line, you have something like an 80% or 90% chance with the opponents at the baseline and your team at the NVZ line. Lobbing from defense mode when in trouble, off-balance, or out of position does not allow your team to move to the NVZ line. Because the opponents have plenty of time, they will likely hit an overhead smash. You gain no advantage by hitting a defensive lob because you must stay back. It is better to hit a dink or a drop shot, move forward to the NVZ line, and lob from a neutral position. You don't usually want to lob from an offensive position either because that is when to attack and hit down on the ball. In other words, there is no reason to lob when you could just hit a smash.

Second, as we discussed earlier, defensive position is primarily survival mode. Trying to attempt too much from survival mode often leads to errors. This is as true for the lob as for dinking and volleying. In defensive mode, just get the ball back in play and wait for an easier shot to attempt a lob. This will lead to a higher success rate, winning you more points. Executing a drop shot is at least as easy as a lob from a defensive position and a safer alternative. When executed correctly, it allows you to move forward, whereas a defensive lob leads to your team moving backward away from where you want to play.

The Volley vs. Dink Lob

You can lob from a volley or a dink on the backhand or forehand side, meaning there are four possible lob scenarios (lobbing from the forehand dink, forehand volley, backhand dink, or backhand volley). In any situation, remember that it is essential to disguise the lob to retain the element of surprise. This means keeping the shot as similar to the dink or volley as possible. Do not telegraph or advertise the lob with a big backswing. Disguise is a critical element of the lob. Many players begin winding up for the lob too early, signaling their opponents to step back. Know beforehand what you will do but keep the lob similar to the dink or volley motion to maintain the element of surprise. Most opponents will not react in time to retrieve the ball if it goes over their heads.

In addition to maintaining disguise, you should determine your preferred lob scenario and primarily practice and utilize your strong suit. For example, are you more comfortable hitting a backhand lob or a forehand, out of the air or off the bounce? Practice lobbing from both sides and take note of which you prefer. Know your strengths and lob from your preferred side (forehand/backhand) and preferred stroke (dink/volley). This helps gain confidence and increase your success rate.

Finally, don't overdo it. Once you have a reputation as a lobber, players expect it and step back, making it easier for them to smash the ball at your feet. The element of surprise is one of the most critical aspects of lobbing successfully, so make sure to retain it. Choose the time to lob wisely, so opponents don't know when it's coming and don't expect it. It depends on the opponents but using it at opportune moments 2 to 4 times per game is probably a good starting point, so you don't overdo it.

Differences from the Dink or Volley

We have determined that keeping the lob as similar to the volley or dink as possible is best. However, it has to be different somehow; otherwise, it wouldn't be a distinct shot. So what exactly changes when hitting a lob vs. volleying or dinking? Two things primarily: paddle angle and follow through. After deciding to lob, disguise the shot as long as possible by keeping the shot preparation similar. At the last second, change the paddle to a more open or upward angle, so the ball travels higher. The other component, followthrough, means swinging with more force and follow through than for a dink or volley. This will give the ball the distance it needs to land within a few feet of the opponent's baseline. These are really the only two elements that change. Keep the lob as simple as possible by not changing anything else. This will allow you to hit the lob more consistently, in addition to disguising it better.

Placement

A few placement tips will help increase your lob success rate. In order of importance, here are the places to aim. Remember that I recommend this for tournament play, not necessarily recreational play. In recreational play, why not lob over the better player? It is better practice and requires your lobs to be perfect. Is winning a recreational game really more important than improving? Not backing away from the challenge will make you a better player (in addition to making you fewer enemies). Here are some tips for locations to aim in tournament play with that in mind.

1. Over the Slower, Shorter, Injured, or Weaker Player

2. Over the Backhand side

3. Crosscourt

4. Into the Sun & Wind

It is no secret that lobbing over the slower, shorter, injured, or weaker player raises success. At the risk of instantly alienating my female readership and sounding like a chauvinist pig, the woman is typically the player being lobbed in mixed doubles. Even when playing men's or women's doubles tournaments, identify the player who will have a more challenging time retrieving or smashing the lob. Every player has their strength and weakness, so exploit the opponents' weaknesses as much as possible while utilizing your own strengths.

It is also no secret that most players hit an overhead better on their forehand side. For this reason, lobbing over the backhand side is an effective strategy. Even if the lob is imperfect, the overhead will not come back as fast when hit from the backhand side. Be careful when lobbing the player whose backhand is in the middle, though. Usually, this means their partner's forehand is also in the middle, allowing them to move back and hit a forehand overhead. Lobbing over the player whose backhand is not in the middle takes their partner out of the equation.

Many players also have difficulty controlling the lob down the line because of the shorter distance. Therefore, lobbing crosscourt to the backhand side is an effective strategy for gaining margin of error. Hitting the lob crosscourt lessens this risk of hitting long because it is further to the baseline. Remember, though, lobbing crosscourt means hitting closer to the sideline, so give yourself plenty of margin for error on the sideline as well.

Hitting lobs with the opponents looking into the sun is probably the strategy that loses the most friends. But it is a valuable weapon to keep in the arsenal for a big point or two at a critical juncture of a game. Even after an imperfect lob, opponents looking straight into the sun often cannot see the ball well enough to smash it. Like hitting crosscourt, lobbing into the wind is also practical because it prevents lobs from sailing out. Because the wind is pushing against you, though, remember that you must swing considerably harder, as lobbing softly into the wind is a recipe for disaster.

Identifying the Right Time

Identifying the right time to lob can be as important as other aspects of lobs we discussed. There are two primary times to lob. Look to pull the trigger in these situations.

Newton's law of motion states that an object at rest tends to stay at rest and an object in motion tends to stay in motion. I believe pickleball players are the same. Whether they realize it or not, a dinking player expects to continue dinking. Therefore they expect the next shot will be a dink for the simple reason that they want it to be a dink. This is especially true after hitting several dinks in a row. As a result, the paddle's ready position begins falling lower and lower, and their preparation becomes lazy. Exploit this tendency by occasionally lobbing after a long dink rally when you know your opponent expects another dink. Chaos, panic, or even complete surrender will often ensue. After a long volley exchange, the same can be said if you prefer lobbing from a volley situation. When you see a low volley that you cannot attack, most opponents will not expect a lob, so it's a great time to do just that.

Identify another lob scenario by looking at the opponent's momentum. What do I mean by this? Imagine a dinking rally where a ball clips the tape and barely rolls over the net. Your opponent must dash into the NVZ, scrambling just to reach the ball in time. Their momentum has carried them forward to retrieve the ball, so it is often difficult for them to return behind the NVZ line in time to hit the next shot. Take advantage of this by lobbing over them or simply driving the ball right at them. Either way, they are at a significant disadvantage because they are still standing in the NVZ line or barely out of it.

Topspin

Lobbing with topspin makes the shot more difficult to retrieve. This is because a ball hit with topspin bounces differently upon impact, skipping and traveling further away from where it was hit. At the risk of sounding like a broken record, perfect the simple shot before attempting the spectacular. Consistently hitting a simple lob is preferable to making mistakes from a more difficult topspin lob.

Being Lobbed

We have discussed the strategies to employ when hitting the lob until this point. Let's now discuss what happens when you or your partner are the ones being lobbed. This includes the strategies/techniques for hitting an overhead smash and what happens when the lob flies over your head.

The Overhead Smash

Ideally, hit an overhead smash when lobbed. This is generally preferable to letting the ball bounce. As the word implies, you get to be aggressive, hit down on the ball, and take time away from the opponents when smashing. However, letting the ball bounce is preferable to hitting an unbalanced or dangerous overhead. Scooting or shuffling back while attempting an overhead is a common cause of injury, as you can lose balance and fall backward. Avoid this scenario by letting the ball bounce and retrieving the ball. Saving one point at all costs is not worth the time and money to heal an injury.

How to Hit

There are two essential techniques to remember when preparing for the overhead. First, turn the shoulders so that your non-hitting hand is in front and raised. Similarly to the return, turning your shoulders allows the entire body, especially your core, to get involved. Players who don't turn their shoulders or have their non-hitting hand raised tend to hit the overhead mainly with their wrists or arms. Hitting with these smaller muscles means a weaker shot and putting undue strain on those individual parts. Using the arms and wrists is not bad, as long as you use them in conjunction with the larger muscles like the legs and torso. Imagine you are winding up by turning sideways, then rapidly unwinding as you hit the overhead smash and return to looking straight forward.

Second, often you must step back to hit the overhead. Turning your shoulders allows you to side-shuffle or karaoke step (look this up if you don't know what it is) while stepping back. Again, moving backward while facing forwards is one of the most dangerous movements in pickleball. Many players lose their balance and fall backward. This has led to wrist, elbow, shoulder, back, and head injuries such as concussions. To stay safe, do not attempt to move backward without turning your shoulders. After turning the shoulders, side shuffle, run, or karaoke-step backward, allowing you to maintain your balance while quickly moving back to hit the overhead smash.

After stepping back:

1. Contact the ball at the highest point possible with the hitting arm fully extended above your head. The contact point should be straight above you or slightly in front.

2. Make sure your non-hitting hand is raised.

3. As you swing, replace your non-hitting hand with the paddle as you rapidly drive through the shot.

4. Swing all the way through, with the paddle finishing ultimately across your body.

Where to Hit

There are a few factors to consider when aiming the overhead. In order of priority, here they are:

1. The Opponent's Feet

2. The Weaker Player

3. Open Spaces

The Opponent's Feet

When hitting an overhead, you often do not have the time or leeway to aim for a specific place on the court. The deeper the lob, the more difficult it is to aim. In this case, simply make sure your overhead is aimed low towards the opponent's feet. An overhead smash directed at the feet is much more difficult to retrieve, and even if it is retrieved, the next ball will often float high, resulting in an easier overhead or attackable ball. On the other hand, an overhead directed toward the opponent's body is easier to retrieve and can even come back as an attack, especially at the higher levels. To maintain the advantage, attack down to the opponent's feet whenever possible.

Aiming for the weaker player is a good strategy, but reserve it for tournament situations. As I mentioned before, to improve your game in recreational play, attack the better player. This will force you to hit a lower, harder overhead, so you become accustomed to higher-level pickleball where even overheads sometimes come back. In a tournament situation, all bets are off. Aim for the weaker player and win by any legal means necessary.

Open Spaces

Many players lob out of desperation (not a strategy we recommend). This means they are scrambling, out of balance, or pulled off the court when they lob. Because they are already scrambling, they often leave large sections of the court open to attack. When the opponents leave any space down the middle, hit there. The margin for error is much higher when hitting down the middle, so this is almost always the best place to aim if it is open. If the opening is down a sideline, proceed with caution; sometimes, this is a good spot, but not always. Personally, when the lob is short, I am more comfortable aiming for the sidelines because I have a better angle to work with. The angle is not as favorable when the lob is deep, so I play it safe by smashing down the middle first. Remember that you do not need to hit a winner from the first overhead. If the first lob is deep, set up the point by hitting an overhead hard down the middle. Often, this results in another shorter lob, and you can continue pressing the advantage. Since you already have the advantage, do not take an unnecessary risk by going for too much too early. Don't give away the advantage by hitting softly, either. Maintain the pressure and wait for the perfect ball that you can put away.

The Non-Attacking Partner

When your partner is hitting the overhead, stay at the NVZ line. In most cases, the opponents will either miss or return the ball high, allowing you to attack the next ball. Scooting back reduces your team's advantage. If the opponents float the ball high, you need to be standing at the NVZ line, ready to attack. You can even move toward the middle sometimes and poach to put even more pressure on the opponents.

When you Cannot Hit an Overhead

Now imagine the opponent lobs. You turn your shoulders, preparing to hit an overhead smash, but the lob flies over your head. What should you do?

The nice thing about preparing to smash by turning your shoulders is that you are already halfway turned. Simply continue turning until your body faces the baseline.

Then, run back to the baseline, never taking your eyes off the ball. Facing forward while running is faster and safer, giving you a better chance of effectively retrieving the lob. The goal now is to run back, maintaining enough distance from the ball so that you can hit a balanced drop shot. Do not lob or drive the ball; the opponents have plenty of time to attack either shot, and you will dig yourself into a deeper hole. Many players claim they don't have time to hit anything except a lob or a drive, but logically, this doesn't make sense. If you have time to hit a lob or drive, you can hit a drop shot - they all take the same amount of time. Being able to hit a drop shot is more of a mindset than anything and gives your team the best chance to return to the NVZ line where pickleball should be played.

When running, make sure not to run straight towards the ball, as you need room to swing. Instead, place enough distance between yourself and the ball so that you can hit a drop shot with your arm extended. Most players prefer to retrieve the lob on their forehand side, so position your body to hit a forehand. But if you prefer a backhand, run back accordingly. Like other shots, it is essential to identify your strength and utilize it whenever possible to raise the percentage of shots made.

After hitting a drop shot, the strategy is essentially the same as the third shot section so refer back for a more detailed explanation. Remember that you are likely moving backward and therefore have to swing harder than a regular drop shot. It is best to run back then step into the drop shot, but sometimes there is not enough time, so you have to adjust your swing accordingly. Ideally, your partner stays at the NVZ line to cover for you if the opponent hits a short ball. Since you are all the way back at the baseline, it's challenging to cover this shot without your partner's help. If your partner stays at the line and you decide to lob, you have just sacrificed them. Do this too many times, and you will need to look for a new partner because they will dump you. If you hit a drop shot, but it floats high, they need to quickly move back before the opponents' attack. The idea here is to quickly take a step back to step into the reset shot instead of stepping back while hitting. Make sure to communicate, though, because they need to know as soon as possible what to do. This way, they know to stay at the line or retreat a little and prepare for the impending attack.

Who Retrieves the Lob

Deciding who retrieves a lob is a crucial split-second decision. However, partner communication - both before the game starts and the second the lob goes up - is critical. There are a few factors to consider when thinking about this.

As stated in the overhead section, it is preferable to hit an overhead smash if you can. If a lob can be attacked, the forehand or the person closest to the ball should smash. In mixed doubles, the male partner often moves over to take the overhead in the middle, both because their overhead is stronger (sorry ladies), they are taller, and because their forehand is typically in the middle.

Before the game, discuss with your partner, who will retrieve lobs that fly over your heads. As a rule of thumb, when the even (right) side partner is lobbed, the odd (left) side partner retrieves the ball. This is because most players' forehand drop shots are stronger than their backhands, especially when retrieving a lob. When the odd (left) side partner is lobbed, it is anybody's ball. The faster, stronger, closer player or the person who sees the lob first should retrieve it. Make sure to communicate as soon as possible, so you don't both go back, run into each other, or neither of you retrieve it. Remember, ideally, one partner stays up at the NVZ line to cover a short ball, so you shouldn't both retreat.

Note that a combination of pre-game and instant partner communication is critical here. Decide beforehand who will retrieve the lob in each scenario, so you have a game plan. However, if the player who is supposed to retrieve the lob is not prepared or does not see it in time, their partner needs to be ready. Just because you have a game plan does not mean you cannot change it or react to the situation. Everything is in flux during a point, so make adjustments as you go. Communicate any changes to your partner on the fly to be on the same page whenever possible.

So what should the non-retrieving partner (the player who remains at the NVZ line) do? There are a couple of factors in determining this. First, it depends on whether you are in the line of fire. What do I mean by this? Let's say you are on the right (even side), and the lob goes over your head with your partner going back to retrieve it. Your body is now blocking your partner's down-the-line drop shot, the easiest shot for them to hit. Typically, you need to move over to the odd (left side of the court) to get out of the way before they hit. After your partner hits the drop shot, they can move straight forward (the closest distance to the NVZ line), allowing them to quickly get back into the point. Prepare to take any short balls, as your partner will likely not be able to return to the NVZ line in time. If you see that your partner's drop shot is successful, you can move towards the middle to pressure the opponents. You can even poach, but you must really trust your partner and know that they will hit a superb drop shot to do this.

Another decision is whether you should retreat a little from the NVZ line when your partner is retrieving the lob. A couple of factors go into this as well. First, how much skill and speed does your partner have? Drop shots are tough enough from a stable position, let alone when your partner runs backward and barely reaches the ball. Sometimes your partner will hit the drop shot too high. Look at what kind of ball they hit and either scoot back or stay at the NVZ line accordingly. If they haven't hit one successfully all day, you probably want to take a step back to prepare. Instead of scooting back automatically, though, as much as possible only scoot back after verifying the drop will go high. This puts pressure on the opponents if your partner hits a successful drop shot because you will be ready for the next ball.

Second, whether to retreat from the NVZ is determined by how well the opponents hit the lob. If your partner recognizes the lob quickly, moves back, has plenty of time to hit a controlled drop shot, and is still inside the baseline when hitting, there is often no need to retreat. You can reasonably expect that they will hit a good shot. On the other hand, if your partner reacts slowly to the lob and barely gets there, is behind the baseline when they reach the ball, or is flailing/panicking, the chances of them hitting a successful drop shot diminish significantly. Take a step or two back to buy yourself some time and protect your good looks. But remember that when the opponent makes contact, you need to be stopped, in balance, and leaning forward.

If you decide to step back in either situation, do it as quickly as possible. As soon as you see the drop shot going high, step back and get ready. The attack is coming. Make sure you lean forward, even in defensive mode. Stepping back quickly allows you to step into the next shot rather than stepping back while hitting. In addition, make sure you do not retreat too far. Going all the way back gives your opponents too much space. Retreat only to buy yourself a little more time but don't give the opponents the entire court by joining your partner at the baseline.

Looking Back

As the non-retrieving partner, make sure to look back at what your partner is doing in all these situations. Not looking back means you are guessing where they are going to hit. Make sure you look back so you do not get in the way of their shot and so that you can prepare for the next ball early. If your partner hits an excellent drop shot, take a step towards the middle to put pressure on the opponents and if they get it too high, be ready to poach. Adjusting to your partner's shot by looking back is a helpful tool to help you make slight adjustments along the way.

Conclusion

Lobbing is a high-level part of pickleball that can be used effectively when done well. Remember to only lob in a neutral or offensive position because your opponents have too much time to step back and smash when you lob from a defensive position. Identify your preferred lobbing shot (forehand vs. backhand, dink vs. volley) to raise the percentage of successful lobs you hit. When smashing, turn your shoulders and use your whole body instead of individual parts. And if the lob goes over your head, make sure to hit a drop shot, not another lob, to give yourself a chance to get back into the point. Like every other shot, get out there and practice so that you can perfect lobbing, smashing, and retrieving lobs.

Chapter 10

The Mental Game

By Daniel

The mental game is often the only difference between good and great players. Some people have mental toughness or the ability to not break down under pressure. Pickleball is even more of a mental game because you must actually finish the game on your serve, where you start the point at a disadvantage; you cannot simply get a lead then coast to victory or run out the clock. Some people just seem to have that ability to finish games, while others don't. Here are some tips for improving your mental game and becoming a better, mentally stronger pickleball player.

Playing To Win

Playing to win, rather than playing not to lose, is a subtle yet crucial difference between players. Playing to win means taking calculated risks, going for shots when wise, and playing the same way throughout the entire game. Playing not to lose means hoping the opponents will make a mistake and do the work for you. Playing to win is easy towards the beginning of a game. It's in the final stages of a match when nerves become a factor that players start playing not to lose, hoping the opponents will give away the game. Even at the pro level, I have to admit that we are sometimes guilty. Try to continue playing the way that brought you success. Focus on each shot and each point rather than the overall score. Don't play in fear; play with confidence and attempt to finish the game.

Positivity

The power of positivity cannot be understated. There is so much pressure sometimes felt, not from the opponents but from yourself or your own teammate, that you get nervous and start playing poorly. Instead, become a good partner and a better player by remaining positive no matter the situation. In my experience, I have never seen a situation where negativity improves a partner's performance but have witnessed the opposite countless times. Not only does positivity make pickleball more fun, but it also gives you the best chance of winning, so try to always stay positive.

Negativity also gives the opponents' an edge by giving them something to exploit. They see your team's adverse reaction and know they are in your head. Don't let them have that mental advantage. Instead, stay positive, letting them know that your team is working together, mentally tough, and will not crack under pressure.

Perspective

Personally speaking, the proper perspective also gives me a mental advantage. What do I mean by that? I remind myself that this is just a game intended to be fun. There are many things outside of pickleball to be thankful for, like family, friends, and life. I have been a national champion a half dozen times and in national finals about a dozen times. Pickleball is just a game. In any circumstance you find yourself in, remember it's just pickleball, and you are blessed and fortunate to have the health, ability, and time to be out there. I'm not saying you should stop caring. I am super competitive and hate losing as much as anyone else. But reminding yourself to have fun can strangely loosen you up and help you play better. You won't get as nervous when losing isn't that big of a deal. Remember, keep everything in perspective, and above all else, have fun! I guarantee you will play better.

Never Give Up

The great thing about pickleball's current scoring system (for better or worse, there is talk of going to rally scoring) is that no lead is insurmountable. No matter how desperate the situation, never give up. At every level, there are stories of teams coming back from extreme deficits to win the game, match, or even tournament, so don't give up or stop giving it your all until the game is truly over. Unfortunately, too many players don't believe they can make a comeback, so guess what happens? They never do.

Ignore the Opponents

Sometimes opponents intentionally try to get in your head by yelling every time they win a point, questioning calls, cheating, trying to distract you, or just being plain rude. Trust me, I have seen it all. They want you to take the bait and become flustered. Just ignore them. If you choose to say something, say it once, then forget about it, or say it after beating them. Your opponents' actions should not matter as long as you let your pickleball speak for itself, so beat them and don't let their attitude or shenanigans affect your play or emotions. That is typically the best answer to a bully. If you are someone who actually responds well to a rude player, make sure you use it positively. Too many players let their anger overcome them, and they focus on trying to hit their opponent or get even, rather than taking care of business by just winning the game. Even if you are annoyed, try not to show any negative emotion and play the same way you always do.

Etiquette

Contrarily, winning while being nice can be maddening for opponents. They have no reason to be upset because you were so polite but recognize that they just got their butts handed to them nonetheless. Let your pickleball do the talking rather than your mouth, frustration, or anger. Be the person who says "nice shot" when it's true, and pick up the ball and hit it straight back to them, no matter what. Kicking the ball or rolling it under the net is not good etiquette, so don't be that person. Instead, kill them with kindness; this is by far the most satisfying way to win. Besides, being the person most people don't mind losing means winning more games. Etiquette also helps keep all the emotions on the court and helps me stay friends with an opponent even after a competitive match.

Timeouts

I struggled in deciding where to talk about timeouts in this book because they apply to all areas but eventually decided that it should be part of the mental game. Pickleball is a game of momentum. Teams often win several points in a row, then struggle later to convert side-outs into points. The key to taking effective timeouts is recognizing the beginning of a momentum shift in favor of your opponents and stopping it by taking a timeout. Many players lose 4 or 5 points before taking a timeout; this is too late. Especially towards the end of an important game, if your opponents win 2 or 3 points in a row on the serve, immediately take a timeout. If it's a really crucial part of a game (like 9-9 in the third game), take a timeout after losing just one or two points. It's better to use all your timeouts than save them and lose the game.

Most players take timeouts when their opponents are serving to stop their momentum and prevent them from scoring more points. However, consider taking a timeout when serving if your team is ahead and struggling to finish the game. Take a moment to cool down, think about the strategy, and win the game. Icing the returner can work as effectively as icing the server.

Smart Pickleball

Finally, a component of mental toughness is just staying smart. Many players continue with a losing strategy for far too long, effectively going down with a sinking ship. Instead, keep talking with your partner and noticing tendencies or patterns in your opponents' play. In every situation, think about going for the smart shot, not the spectacular shot or the one that will impress the crowd. Pickleball is all about making fewer errors than your opponents, and when they know you won't make any, they will become frustrated. Create an impenetrable wall that they cannot breakthrough, and they will overhit, take risks and make mistakes. Consistently hit the opponents' feet, only attack from an offensive position, serve/return deep, and just play smart, high percentage pickleball. I guarantee you will win more points, and therefore games.

Chapter 11

Your Pickleball Top 10

By Scott

We want to challenge you to perform an exercise. Pickleball is all about the relationships and the memories we make. So create your own list of your 10 favorite pickleball memories. You can update the list as you go. It's nice to look back on all the tournaments, moments, friendships, and memories and appreciate just how fortunate we are. As an example, here are my and Daniel's top 10 pickleball related memories:

Scott's Top 10

10. Winning the Battle of the Sexes. Unlike the controversial tennis version, this was legitimate as Simone and I were both the undisputed best players in our respective categories at the time. We dressed up in 70s attire and had a live crowd and PPV audiences (the first time in pickleball). Susan and I did a dance routine between the doubles and singles matches, while Morgan Evans and Alex Hamner did a fabulous job announcing, almost stealing the show! People asked us if we threw the first game of the doubles and singles to make it more exciting, but the answer is definitely no. Those ladies are fabulous players and were on fire, tearing us apart in the first game. I still feel fortunate that I pulled out both matches. Besides, throwing a game is not in my nature. Follow the link to the videos if you want to see the real battles of the sexes.

https://www.youtube.com/watch?v=OBFRIhhk40U

https://www.youtube.com/watch?v=EXZAqLmY_9I

9. Winning the Italian Open with my son Jon despite fracturing my wrist during the winner's bracket final. The indoor surface felt like an ice skating rink, and I fell attempting an Ernie. Unfortunately, we didn't win another point and lost the match. We fought back through the opportunity bracket, though, and fought our way back to play the Spanish team of Ernesto and Carlos (the European champions) for the gold in front of a pro-Europe crowd. Jon had not played pickleball for very long but came into his own that day and carried me to the gold medal. The Bainbridge Cup the previous day was also a total blast as the whole Italy pickleball trip.

8. Watching Daniel and Matt Staub win the gold at the Tournament of Champions in 2016, after one of their opponents (no names mentioned) guaranteed on Social Media that he was going to win the tournament. In the gold medal match, Daniel and Matt crushed them 11-2, 11-3. So much for guarantees, and fun to see Daniel continue his run at the top of the pickleball world.

7. Taking people on pickleball trips all over the world. So far, I've done Spain, Italy, Thailand, Japan, St. Croix, and several places in Mexico and have heard several participants claim it was the best trip of their life. The trips combine my life passions of pickleball, adventure, family, food, and engaging with people from different cultures. It does not get any better than that, and I am constantly ticking off my travel bucket list.

6. The Streaks--Winning 12 straight events at Nationals, including 2 triple crowns and 10 straight at TOC, including 3 triple crowns from 2015-2017, and thereby setting some records that may never be broken was an unbelievably fun ride.

5. Daniel winning his first Nationals Men's Open Doubles in 2015 with Mattew Blom. He won gold in doubles and silver in singles in addition to two golds at TOC, making him the best player in the world at the time. Personal success is fantastic, but seeing your kids excel is about us as good as it gets. Pickleball Rocks named us the Co-Players of the Year award. It was an indescribable thrill beyond my wildest imagination to be the best in the world at something and get to share that with my son.

4. Winning the 50+ singles gold medal at nationals in 2016 the same day Daniel won the 19+ and his grandfather won the 85+ singles. My stepfather was the only player in the bracket, but that doesn't matter. It is the only time 3 generations have won gold on the same day at nationals and will also likely be a record that stands forever.

3. Daniel and I becoming national champions for the first time on the same day in 2014. You can read the introduction section for the details, but to become a national champion and get to share that with Daniel was a feeling I can't even begin to describe.

3. I couldn't choose, so this one is tied for third. Watching Daniel win the 2017 Nationals Gold medal with Matt Wright (He plays well with partners named Matt). In the winner's bracket final, they lost to Kyle Yates and Wes Gabrielsen, then came back to double dip them and win it all. To this day, it is still one of the best matches I have ever seen, but CBS tragically cannot find the recording.

2. Winning the Bend Regional tournament in 5.0 men's doubles with Daniel. Playing with the young guys was tough. Almost every match went 3 games. Against the Canadian team of Marco and Steve Deakin, we were down 6-0 in game 3 before coming back to win 11 straight points. Then we lost in the winner's bracket final to Wes and Brian Ashworth before coming back to double dip them for the gold. It was so fun that it almost (emphasis on almost) didn't matter whether we won or lost. Brian later reminded me that they had age groups for a reason, and I needed to play with people my own ******* age.

1. The relationships we have made along the way. My friend John Anderson reminded me several years ago that it is all about relationships. Regrettably, in the heat of the battle, I have occasionally forgotten this sage wisdom and have had to later apologize a few times when I forget. Despite this, I am blessed to meet thousands of people worldwide through pickleball. Some have become friends for life, and I share unforgettable memories with many others.

Daniel's Top 10

10. Seeing pickleball courts built in Japan. Recently, a few people have been building private pickleball courts in Japan. I never thought I would see the day when people would actually start building dedicated pickleball courts, so it's exhilarating and a sign that pickleball is growing here like crazy.

9. Starting pickleball in Kenya. After university, I went for entirely different reasons than pickleball when I lived in Kenya. In fact, I hadn't even started playing pickleball yet. So returning to Kenya for pickleball and seeing how excited people became brought things full circle. It is incredible how seemingly unrelated experiences in my life become connected and are helpful in whatever I do next.

8. Bringing pickleball to China. In 2019, I had the opportunity to visit China for 2 weeks and train 15-20 coaches who would subsequently take it to schools around Southern China. Not only were the players excited about pickleball, but they also showed me a great time (taking me to street markets and late-night karaoke), and we became fast friends. This solidified my belief that "pickleball diplomacy" can bring unfriendly countries together and become a force for unity.

7. Running pickleball trips with my dad and brother. It is not often that families work together (we have our struggles too). But running a successful travel business with my family is one of my proudest accomplishments. Travel remains one of my biggest passions in life, so much so that I have another travel company called Active Travel Japan.

6. Founding the Japan Open. I came up with the idea for the Japan Open with my friend Makoto. Sadly, he passed away suddenly in 2019 from a brain hemorrhage, just months before the tournament. We ran the tournament in his honor and managed to have a successful event. He was a founding member of pickleball in Japan, someone I could not have done it without. In addition, he was one of my best friends. I have since given up running the tournament myself (the Japan Pickleball Association took it over), but it makes me happy that the tournament continues Makoto's legacy.

5. Winning nationals in men's open doubles, 2017. By 2017, my other businesses were becoming busier, leaving me less time to train for pickleball. Although no one counted me out, I was certainly not a favorite to win tournaments anymore. I enjoy being the underdog, though. Playing one of the best matches I have ever played on the biggest stage was a memory I cherish forever.

4. 2015 TOC to 2016 US Open. This was the period of my best run at national tournaments. From the 2015 Tournament of Champions onward, I won 2 golds and 1 silver in men's doubles, 1 gold in mixed doubles, and 1 gold, 1 silver, and 1 bronze in men's singles. It was the best I have ever played, and no one will be able to take those wins and championships away.

3. Tournament of Champions 2019. By 2019, it's safe to say that no one expected me to win national-level tournaments. I was dangerous and could surprise good teams, though. Matt Wright had agreed to team up with me 2 years earlier when we won nationals (that's how crazy finding a partner has gotten). Although Matt and I lost in the third game of the finals to Ben Johns and Kyle Yates (the undisputed best team in the world), we beat them once and showed the world a great match. I wanted to win for Makoto, who had passed away just a month before, but I fell just short.

2. Opportunities and Friendships. Like my dad's last section, the opportunities and friendships created through pickleball have been nothing short of incredible. It is no understatement to say it has changed my life. From a catered trip to Taiwan, the guest of honor in Singapore, and friends worldwide, I can no longer imagine my life without pickleball. Most of my income is now tied to pickleball, so maybe it's best not to imagine a life without pickleball!

1. Seeing pickleball grow in Japan. During the pickleball trips to Japan, we play with local clubs as we travel around the country. Seeing a gym packed full of pickleball players from around the world having fun, I always take a minute to breathe it in. "I started this," I often say to myself. It reminds me of my purpose, the motivation behind all the miles flown and late nights. Of course, I couldn't have done it by myself, but it feels good to be the person who kicked off and facilitated the whole process.

Conclusion

By Scott

We hope you enjoyed the book. I have a completely new appreciation for authors and the amount of time they put into their work. I can also say that having the opportunity to be involved in so many ventures, most of them involving pickleball, I have never had more fun doing business in my life. Since the work involves pickleball, the line between work and play has become so blurry that I can't tell which I'm doing (though it always goes better if I tell Susan I'm working). I love all my "offices" (i.e, pickleball courts) around the country, where I get to improve and share my craft.

We are genuinely grateful, and though it has not been a perfect ride, we can attest to the fact that following your dreams is never the wrong answer. We are grateful for the role that pickleball has played and hope you are equally blessed.

If you are interested in combining pickleball and vacation, I want to invite you to join us on one of our pickleball trips. We always have a blast teaching pickleball, eating wonderful food, and relaxing in an exotic location. To check out our upcoming trips, visit PickleballTrips.com.

Remember it's all about fun and friends. Keep on swinging, live without regrets, stop procrastinating, never grow up, play hard, and try to be the best you can be.

God bless.

Scott and Daniel Moore

HighPerformancePickleballAcademy.com

PickleballTrips.com